MW01199106

There is Hope!
Psalm 25:4,5

Ricki Elds

I Could Not Save the Little Bird

ADDICTION:

A Mother's Birds-eye View
and The Lessons She Learned

Ricki Elks

WESTBOW
PRESS
A DIVISION OF THOMAS NELSON
& ZONDERVAN

Copyright © 2015 Ricki Elks.

All rights reserved. No part of this book may be used or reproduced by any means, graphic, electronic, or mechanical, including photocopying, recording, taping or by any information storage retrieval system without the written permission of the publisher except in the case of brief quotations embodied in critical articles and reviews.

Scripture taken from the Holy Bible, NEW INTERNATIONAL VERSION®. Copyright © 1973, 1978, 1984 by Biblica, Inc. All rights reserved worldwide. Used by permission. NEW INTERNATIONAL VERSION® and NIV® are registered trademarks of Biblica, Inc. Use of either trademark for the offering of goods or services requires the prior written consent of Biblica US, Inc.

Scripture taken from the New King James Version. Copyright © 1979, 1980, 1982 by Thomas Nelson, Inc. Used by permission. All rights reserved.

Scripture taken from the King James Version of the Bible.

Scripture quotations taken from the Holy Bible, New Living Translation, Copyright © 1996, 2004. Used by permission of Tyndale House Publishers, Inc., Wheaton, Illinois 60189. All rights reserved.

Interior Graphics/Art Credit: Cynthia M Gillim for image #2 (girl spinning plates)

WestBow Press books may be ordered through booksellers or by contacting:

WestBow Press
A Division of Thomas Nelson & Zondervan
1663 Liberty Drive
Bloomington, IN 47403
www.westbowpress.com
1 (866) 928-1240

Because of the dynamic nature of the Internet, any web addresses or links contained in this book may have changed since publication and may no longer be valid. The views expressed in this work are solely those of the author and do not necessarily reflect the views of the publisher, and the publisher hereby disclaims any responsibility for them.

Any people depicted in stock imagery provided by Thinkstock are models, and such images are being used for illustrative purposes only. Certain stock imagery © Thinkstock.

ISBN: 978-1-4908-8111-9 (sc)
ISBN: 978-1-4908-8112-6 (hc)
ISBN: 978-1-4908-8110-2 (e)

Library of Congress Control Number: 2015908053

Print information available on the last page.

WestBow Press rev. date: 06/17/2015

Contents

I Could Not Save the Little Bird

I tried to save the little bird
That fell from the big oak tree,
But I could not save the little bird.
What was wrong with me?

I tried to save my mother,
But day by day she cried.
I could not save my father
No matter how hard I tried.

I tried to save my daughter;
I tried to save my son;
Day by day my heart did ache,
For I had saved no one.

I finally cried, "Dear Father,
What is wrong with me?
I cannot save the ones I love
Or the bird beneath the tree."

So, I gave to Him the ones I love
And sat beneath the tree
And realized that day by day
All I can save is me.

—Ricki Elks

Acknowledgments

To my family and friends:

Larry: Marriage is difficult in the best of circumstances, and today's statistics prove that few are willing to endure the struggles and challenges. We faced many battles, but you stood with me. For that and much more, you are my champion. It is indeed an honor to be your wife.

Renee, Leigh Anna, Joshua, and Ryan: I thank God for trusting me to be your mother and stepmother. I also thank you and God for forgiveness, grace, and love when I did not always get it right.

A special thank you to William Glen Criswell (Uncle Glen) for your beautiful bird pictures.

Larry Elks, my husband, thank you also for drawing the perfect bird icon.

For the advice and encouragement of so many dear friends, I am very grateful.

Introduction

If you are holding this book, you may be feeling pain that is similar to pain I felt not so many years ago. I stood in the self-help section of a bookstore looking for a publication to give me answers. I had loved ones who needed saving, and I would do anything to save them. (I believed I had proven that over and over.) By then, I was realizing my best wasn't good enough; my life and the lives of my loved ones were getting worse, not better. The latest in a long line of crises was that my youngest child had turned to drugs. It felt like I was helplessly watching him drown.

I remember that as I scanned the book titles I thought, "I need a book written by someone who has been where I am now." My situation was urgent. I needed help; I needed answers! I wanted an author who had been where I was. He or she could tell me how they had survived and what they had learned. My friends were growing weary of hearing about my challenges and fears. I wanted to find an author who would feel like a friend but would not grow weary. I didn't find any such book. The book you are holding is the one for which I was searching.

I will share with you from my heart some of my heartbreaks and many of my mistakes. I'll share how my lowest point led me to my greatest victory. I'll share how I found hope and a bounty of answers that outnumbered even the questions I had that day in the bookstore. Our journey together will begin slowly and intensify as we progress. It will parallel the learning process I experienced. Some names in my story have been changed to respect the individuals' privacy.

Before we move on, it is important to emphasize that I have no formal training in behavioral counseling or in the area of drug and alcohol abuse. There are some great books written by the experts. I have read many of them, and you, too, could benefit from them. Over the years, I have also been fortunate to receive much wise counsel from behavioral experts. You may want to consider seeking this option as well. My *only* credentials are those of a mother who has been there. To quote a Romanian proverb: "Only the foolish learn from experience—the wise learn from the experience of others." So, let's just say I have learned a few things over the years, and I am willing to share them in the hope of saving you some painful lessons.

I Lived in Constant Fear That One of My Plates Would Fall

I finally made an appointment to see a counselor. He asked me why I was there. I told him I felt like a circus performer I had seen who could keep seven plates spinning at once on top of seven thin rods. I told him that's who I had become in my life—a circus performer running back and forth giving all the people I love a spin. I would help and love on one of my "plates" and then run to the opposite end to save a wobbling one before it crashed. I lived in constant fear that one of my plates would fall and that it would certainly be my fault. "It's getting harder and harder," I confessed. I told the counselor I felt I was watching my son drown. "I'm here to ask you how to save my son," I said. My marriage and all the rest of my plates were wobbling, but my child was on his way to the floor!

When the counselor finally spoke, I was confused by what he said: "First, let's talk about you." Much later, I understood.

As we spend time together through this book, I hope you will allow yourself to think about more than your loved ones who need to be saved. I hope you will think about *you*. Let's begin.

Chapter 1

What's the Truth?

Why did the counselor want to talk about me? Can you imagine running up to a lifeguard and shouting, "Help! My son is drowning!"

What would you think if the lifeguard responded, "First, let's talk about you." You would probably think the lifeguard hadn't heard you or had missed the sense of urgency. I was thinking the same thing right then.

I resigned myself to cooperate with the process; I decided I would give the counselor a rundown of my life. Then, I thought, he would understand how I had messed up my child. At the end of the hour, he would be able to give me the answer on how to save my son. So I talked about me.

I talked about the tension I experienced as a child in my family's home as my dad suffered from alcoholism. I shared about growing up with feelings of unworthiness. I shared about my previous marriage and divorce that left me feeling rejected and like a failure. The list of failures and proofs of my unworthiness as a person and as a mother flowed from my mouth as the tears flowed from my eyes. Then, the hour was over, and the counselor said, "Would you come back next Tuesday at this same time."

I was expecting a solution, not another appointment. I reminded him of why I was there (in case he had missed the point). "What about my son?" I asked. "What can I do?"

He responded, "If I told you today what I think you should do, I don't believe you could accept it. We'll talk again next week."

When you are busy "spinning plates" or trying to save others, there is little time to think about yourself. I had not really thought about myself in a long time. What had the counselor heard me say that made him believe I wasn't ready for his answer? Was there something in my past that influenced my relationship skills? Couldn't the counselor hear I loved my child and wanted to save him? I made another appointment. But I left with more questions than I had before our session.

I believe those unanswered questions were possibly the greatest result of the counseling sessions. Those questions were responsible for the journey I began, a journey for answers to questions, starting with "Who am I?" I looked for the truth.

Pause for

a Bird's-Eye View

Early in my journey for answers, I was tempted to quit. I often didn't like what I was being told. For example, I was frustrated when the counselor asked me to return for a second visit. As I left the first appointment without a solution, I was tempted not to return. That would have been a big mistake! You may feel the same way before you reach the end of this book. Please stay with me until the end. I don't want you to miss the answers you need. Let's continue.

Question 1 on Truth: Who Am I?

Remember trying to "find X" in algebra? Maybe you are like me and have forgotten more algebra than you remember. I do recall that if we were looking for X, first we had to take what truth we did know and start there.

What's the truth about me? And about you?

Where does someone find the truth? Our country began by identifying certain truths. The Declaration of Independence says, "We hold these truths to be self-evident, that all men are created equal, that they are endowed by their Creator with certain unalienable Rights, that among these are Life, Liberty and the pursuit of Happiness." I thought that if this approach was good enough for our forefathers, then it was a good enough way for me to start.

I looked into those truths that were supposed to be "self-evident." If all of us were created and given rights by our Creator—rights for life, liberty, and the pursuit of happiness—why was I living as if those truths were not so evident? What had I missed?

I decided it was up to me to learn about my rights. So, I picked up the Creator's resource book (the Bible) and began my quest for the answer to my first question: "Who am I?" I found certain truths of the Creator to be self-evident. Throughout this book I will be sharing these truths as they relate to questions I had. Here are some of these truths and related lessons that I gathered from them that answered my first question, "Who am I?"

Self-Evident Truths

Genesis 1:1: "In the beginning, God created the heavens and the earth."

Lesson: The search for truth begins with God, our Creator.

Genesis 1:27: "So God created mankind in his own image, in the image of God he created them; male and female he created them."

Lesson: God made me.

Psalm 139:13, 14: "For you created my inmost being; you knit me together in my mother's womb. I praise you because I am fearfully and wonderfully made; your works are wonderful, I know that full well."

Lesson: God put thought into making me, and I'm special.

Jeremiah 29:11: "'For I know the plans I have for you,' declares the Lord, 'plans to prosper you and not to harm you, plans to give you hope and a future.'"

Lesson: *God created me with a plan (a good plan) in mind for my life.*

So, what went wrong? Is that what you are asking? If God had specially created me with a good plan in mind, then something must have gone astray, right? *Right!* To be spinning plates and rescuing loved ones does not seem like a good plan.

Pause for

a Bird's-Eye View

As I am preparing this book, I cannot quit thinking about you. Here I am, talking about God and quoting from the Bible, and I am wondering how you feel about that. If you subscribe to a different religion or no religion, I hope you can accept, as have innumerable scholars in various walks of life, that the Bible is full of sound guidance. I am not a theologian. I am simply sharing from my heart. I can only share what I know, what has helped, and what I believe can help you no matter your base. If I shared inaccurately while trying to be politically correct, I would be a liar due to the omission of my truth as a Christian.

For those of you who are Christians: You may have lived like I did for much of my life. I went to church, and I read the Bible a little. I said I knew God, but I didn't live my life as if I really knew Him. There is a saying: "To know, and not to do, is not to know." Therefore, while I said I knew God, did I really know Him?

Perhaps, you have read the Bible, but you somehow missed His treasures of truth or their relevance to your situation. A reminder, along with some shared revelations, may be just what you need to form a battle plan.

So, from wherever you are starting, I hope you have a desire to continue with me. You came here looking for answers. You may be desperately seeking answers. It is my hope you will find them within these pages. I believe you will. Now, where were we?

Question 2 on Truth: What Went Wrong?

I repeat my previous thought: *If God had especially created me with a good plan in mind, what went wrong?* Maybe *I* got in the way.

A popular character in comedic movies and sitcoms is the controlling mother who wants to overly nurture her adult children. There are shows with mothers who think their sons haven't picked the right fiancé or wife, and the mothers try to "help" resolve the problem. These mothers may be cooking and cleaning for their adult children and even picking out their clothes. Often these women are following their adult children around while giving them unsolicited advice and pointing out mistakes. These maternal busybodies sometimes justify their own actions with "They need me." If these mothers are chastised for their overbearing attention, they may respond, "Can I help it if I just love too much?"

Sure, we laugh at these parents in the movies and on television, but is it so funny when it happens in life? When it happens, is it because the adult children need the help, or is it sometimes because the parents need to be needed?

When I was a teenager, I wrote a poem about an obsessive garden weed. When I found and read the poem several years ago, I marveled at the strong personal insight it seems to display, even though I was young then. Can you love too strong? If love is too strong, is it actually some type of need, and if so, is that healthy?

He Loved Too Strong

There was a weed
Who lived alone;
The touch of love
He'd never known.

And he was sad,
Until one day
A lovely rose
Grew there in May.

His love for her
He could not hide;
He always stayed
Close by her side.

He held her strong,
Would not let go.
She could never leave,
For he loved her so.

He held so tight
Rose lost her breath;
He loved so much
It caused her death.

Then grew the weed
Again alone;
The touch of love
He once had known.

Another rose
Grew there next May.
The weed looked at her,
Then looked away.

His kind of love
He knew was wrong.
Some love too little;
He loved too strong.

—Ricki Elks

As I shared my life's story with the counselor, perhaps he perceived some indicators that I was a parent who tried to save others due to an internal need or character flaw that had developed through the years. Did he surmise that I had parented from a place of need due to feelings of rejection, unworthiness, or being unloved? On the outside, was I a fighter, fighting to save the ones I loved, while on the inside I was weak, desperate, and needy?

Yes, I do believe my weaknesses and my lack of knowledge about how to overcome them most definitely got in the way of the good plan the Creator had for my life.

In addition to my personal weaknesses, what else could have pushed my life so far off track from what was planned for me? Again, I went searching in the Word of the Creator for more truths.

Self-Evident Truths

Romans 3:23: "For all have sinned and fall short of the glory of God."

Lesson: We have a sinful nature that tends to mess up God's perfect plan.

John 16:33: "I have told you these things, so that in me you may have peace. In this world you will have trouble. But take heart! I have overcome the world."

Lesson: Bad news: Trouble happens in our world. Good news: We have help.

Genesis 3:6 (NLT): "The woman was convinced. She saw that the tree was beautiful and its fruit looked delicious, and she wanted the wisdom it would give her. So she took some of the fruit and ate it. Then she gave some to her husband, who was with her, and he ate it, too."

Lesson: Bad news: The Enemy lies to us to keep us from God's perfect plan. Good news: We get to choose. More bad news: Sometimes we make bad choices.

⸻❀⸻

Genesis 3:24: "After he drove the man out, he placed on the east side of the Garden of Eden cherubim and a flaming sword flashing back and forth to guard the way to the tree of life."

Lesson: Bad choices have consequences.

⸻❀⸻

John 10:10: "The thief comes only to steal and kill and destroy; I have come that they may have life, and have it to the full."

Lesson: Bad news: Yes, there is an enemy, the Devil. Good news: We have really good help.

I confess I made some bad choices in my life, many of which were sins. Was one sin to accept my disordered life as it was instead of turning to God's truth earlier? Did I choose to believe the lies of an enemy instead of the truth of the Creator?

The counselor wanted to hear about me, and eventually I figured out why. It is powerful for us to know the truth and know who we are. The Bible starts out in Genesis with "In the beginning, God created ..." And that's where I began my journey for answers. I acknowledged that I have a Creator who created me and had a good plan for me. I saw that as a good foundation for creating the new life I desired—*and* the great life I desired for my loved ones who were also lost in the lies of the Enemy. This was just the beginning!

Who Am I?

Some say I'm an evolved primate
That evolved from a one-celled blob.
I say I'm a special design
Made by a special God.

Some say it was by accident
The way my life began.
I say it was on purpose,
Part of the Creator's plan.

When the question's asked,
It matters not what others do reply;
But it matters much that I know the truth
When I ask myself, "Who am I?"

—Ricki Elks

Chapter 2

Searching for Answers

I find this truth to be self-evident:

> Show me your ways, O Lord, teach me your paths;
> guide me in your truth and teach me, for you are
> God my Savior, and my hope is in you all day long.
> (Psalm 25:4, 5)

Early in my search for answers there was no evidence of profound changes in my life or me. Chaos continued to surround me, and I was still doing my share of plate spinning. Feelings of desperation for my children and my marriage were all consuming.

Still, there was a subtle change. I had taken my Bible off the shelf, and I began to use it to search for answers to the many questions that flooded my thoughts. Also, I felt less alone than I had for so long. I now knew with conviction the Creator of the universe loved my loved ones and me. And since His truths were all written, I knew I could find and receive the answers I needed.

So, I turned to Him, through His Word. My questions began with "How can I have any hope in my life when my loved ones are in danger?" My second question was "Lord, is there any way to rest when the battle is raging all around?" Not only did my life seem hopeless, but also I was exhausted. Plate spinning and trying to rescue others who aren't trying to save themselves will do that to you.

We will look back at the journal I kept when I was searching for the answers to these two questions. You may notice that sometimes I was taken back to previously examined verses and led further into a truth I'd already found. Do you need to know the answer to the question, "How can I have any hope in my life when my loved ones are in danger"?

Finding Hope

I remember an especially tough day. It wasn't hard just because of the negative reports that seemed to come from all directions; it was especially hard because of an overwhelming feeling of hopelessness in my life. I couldn't even imagine how my loved ones could be saved from themselves and their choices. I had no hope.

I remember wishing God could just talk to me and tell me there was a reason to hope. With nowhere to turn, I picked up His book. I said out loud, "So what do you have to say about hope?" I began to search.

I turned to the concordance in the back of the Bible. I looked up "h–o–p–e" and started reading anything I could find on the subject. It was just a few minutes into my search that I found it—a much-needed truth.

Self-Evident Truth

Romans 15:13: "May the God of hope fill you
with all joy and peace as you trust in him, so that
you may overflow with hope by the power of the
Holy Spirit."

Let's look at what I wrote in my journal that day as I studied
this truth:

> *Overflow with hope!* Yes, that's what I need, but
> how does a mom overflow with hope when she's
> been told her son has once again given into a
> self-destructive addiction? Plus, that's just one
> negative report from one offspring this week. My
> heart is so heavy. Sure, I know their choices are
> causing their pain, but it's just so hard watching
> them sink in the quicksand of consequences.
>
> Lord, so You are saying I *can* have hope? How?
> Let me read what You said again. Romans 15:13
> "May the God of hope fill you with all joy
> and peace as you trust in him, so that you may
> overflow with hope by the power of the Holy
> Spirit."
>
> Hmmm, the God of *hope* … You're not only the
> Creator of the universe, the Beginning and the
> End, all-knowing and ever-present, but You are
> also the God of hope! Oh Lord, I need hope, and
> You are the God of hope. I know I have come to
> the right place.

You also say here that You will "fill me with all joy and peace." I could sure use a fill-up of joy and peace. What a deal—a one-stop fill-up of joy AND peace. I want it, but how? " ...as you trust in him, ..." There it is—the price! I can get a fill-up, but I must pay in trust in You. I must trust in You and know my help is coming; my joy and peace are coming. I must know it now before I have even seen it with my eyes. I must feel it now, even while all the negative reports are coming.

Lord, I am remembering something else from Your Word:

Jeremiah 29:11 "For I know the plans I have for you," declares the Lord, "plans to prosper you and not to harm you, plans to give you hope and a future."

You have good plans for me, and You have good plans for my children. And there's that word again—HOPE. You have plans to give me "hope." I believe You are speaking these words to me today just like You spoke them to Jeremiah. There was something else You said through Jeremiah:

Jeremiah 17:7–8 "But blessed is the man who trusts in the Lord, whose confidence is in him. He will be like a tree planted by the water that sends out its roots by the stream. It does not fear when heat comes; its leaves are always green. It has no worries in a year of drought and never fails to bear fruit."

So, the message is the same (of course): "blessed is the man (or woman) who TRUSTS in the Lord." So, if I want green leaves (or joy) and no worries (or peace), I must trust in You.

"…so that you may overflow with hope …" I am smiling already as I reread your promise in Romans 15:13. You have a plan for me and my children—a GOOD plan. I don't have the answers, but You do, and it's a GOOD answer— the perfect answer. I am almost laughing aloud as I am feeling joy and peace. I am overflowing with hope!

"…by the power of the Holy Spirit."

Thank You, Holy Spirit for your wisdom and for hope!

That's what happened. Full of discouragement and with no hope, I picked up the Bible. Hours later, I set down the Creator's book and realized I had recovered something I had lost: my smile. Plus, something stirred inside of me—that something was *hope*.

Later, I searched for the answer to the second question, "Lord, is there any way to rest when the battle is raging all around?" Again, I found the solution for which I searched.

Quest for Rest

The drama continued. The characters included a young man who looked like my son, but acted like a stranger. There was also my daughter, whose tears broke my heart. Other characters were police officers, judges, and directors of rehab programs. Then, there were the phone calls—first from the school, saying my son was expelled; then from the rehab facility, saying he was kicked out of their program. The drama continued for years, and it was my life. I was so tired, but I couldn't rest. Sometimes I didn't know where my loved ones were, and I worried. Other times, I knew where they were, and I worried. The drama was a daily companion.

Sound sleep was rare. I often awakened in the night with feelings of panic and a racing heart and mind. One sleepless night, exhausted, I turned to the Creator to see if He had an answer to my second question: "Lord, is there a way to find rest when the battle is raging all around?"

Again, He took me on a journey through His Word—a journey that led to the answer I needed. It began with me discovering the following:

Self-Evident Truth

Psalm 62:5–6: "Find rest, O my soul, in God alone; my hope comes from Him. He alone is my rock and my salvation; He is my fortress; I will not be shaken."

This is what I wrote at that time:

Something happened today when I read the fifth and sixth verses of Psalm 62, "Find rest, O my soul, in God alone; my hope comes from Him. He alone is my rock and my salvation; He is my fortress; I will not be shaken." It was as if the words just jumped out at me. I had prayed this morning and asked God to help me rest. Then, I read these verses, and it was as if I could almost hear Him speaking to me. It was like He was saying, "Listen up, girl—I have a message for you!" I've been told this is a way God can speak to us (through His Word), and I believe He just spoke to me!

I truly believed God had spoken to me, but I didn't instantly have my question answered. I found myself drawn to the verses my search had produced. I wrote the words down and read them throughout the day for several days. I would wake up in the middle of the night and try to quote the verses. I meditated on them for over a week. Then, I went back to my journal and wrote what I discovered during my searching:

"Find rest, O my soul, in God alone;"

Rest. Ohhh, rest! How we need rest, and how hard it can seem to find it. We need rest, not only for our bodies, but also for our minds and souls.

Sometimes when life seems to be coming at me all at once, I look for a good movie (which can be hard even with over a hundred channels). If I do find one, and I throw in a big bowl of ice cream, then for a short period of time, I almost seem to have found some semblance of rest. I forget my worries until the credits roll, and I realize I have once again added an overabundance to my caloric intake. Other times, I seek this place of rest through music. I can lose myself in the words or the rhythm and rest. On a crazier note, I can even find some type of rest when I throw myself into yard work or crazier yet, housework! All of these escapes can take me to some temporary rest-like place for my mind. The rest I find does not always rest my body or certainly not my soul, and it is only temporary. When the movie is over, the music is silent, and the bowl is empty, the need for rest is unsatisfied. Today, as I reflect on this, I wonder why.

"Find rest, O my soul, *in God alone;*"

God answers my question. It is *in God alone* that I can find the rest that I so desperately desire. This is not just rest; it's rest for my *soul!* When I start the movie as I balance my bowl of vanilla ice cream with chocolate syrup and peanuts (my favorite), am I really so different than someone who turns to substance abuse or another harmful addiction? Are we not all looking for rest in a place other than where it can only truly be found—*in God alone?*

"...my hope comes from Him."

Hope. I just love that word. For so many years, I found it hard to have hope. Now, grant you, it was my fault. Remember me—I had been looking for rest in a good movie and ice cream. Well, it was even worse as I was looking for hope. I was looking for hope within myself! With any ᵇallenge I had with my husband, my thought , "How can *I* fix him." (That never f my children were going down a h, I would follow behind them and wisdom at them just knowing if they were "hit" with the right verse or proverb, they'd stop in their tracks and say, "Oh wise mother, you have changed me! I will never go this way again!" (No, that never worked either!) I could go on and on with examples how over the years I tried to find hope within myself. I would even go to church, and I prayed often. I would even tell God I trusted Him. Sometimes I might even wait a *few* minutes before my mind would start planning a new strategy on how I could fix my problems (a.k.a. my loved ones), and again my hope was in myself. Finally, one day I found myself with so many troubles weighing me down, that I looked up. Then, I cried out, "I cannot fix these problems or these people. Lord, I give them to You!" God must have thought, "FINALLY!" That day was the first step to learning that He is the "God of Hope," and "my hope comes from Him."

"He alone is my rock ..."

If I get this, really get this—"He alone is my rock," I truly believe everything else (rest, hope ... everything I need) will fall into place. HE ALONE IS MY ROCK! In Matthew, in the twenty-fourth verse of the seventh chapter, Jesus says, "Therefore, everyone who hears these words of mine and puts them into practice is like a wise man who built his house on the rock." Then, in the twenty-sixth verse, He says, "But everyone who hears these words of mine and does not put them into practice is like a foolish man who built his house on sand." When I first read these words,

21

I felt pretty smug. I thought, "Well, I'm certainly not like that foolish man! Who would be so stupid to build a house on sand?" Then, I thought about the fact that I had been looking for rest in a movie and a bowl of ice cream; and I didn't feel smug at all. If I *know* He alone is my rock, I will know where to build my house *and* find rest for my soul.

"...and my salvation."

"For God so loved the world that He gave his one and only Son, that whoever believes in Him shall not perish but have eternal life" (John 3:16). Well, then, what's my problem? I *believe*, so I will not perish! I will have eternal life! As life comes at me, I need only to remind myself, "I'm just passing through. This life on earth is temporary, like a split hair compared to the billion trillion plus years of worry-free eternity to come. HE IS MY SALVATION!" In the second verse of the twelfth chapter of Hebrews, it says, "fixing our eyes on Jesus, the pioneer and perfecter of faith. For the joy set before him he endured the cross, scorning its shame, and sat down at the right hand of the throne of God." In every crisis, in every pain, in every fear, if I can fix my eyes upon Jesus and remember that He *loved*, that He *gave* and that He *IS* my salvation, I will most surely rest.

"He is my fortress."

I have wonderful childhood memories of playing chase. I remember the thrill of someone on my

heels as I ran as hard as I could to get to "home."
Home base could be the big oak tree or the swing
set or the front porch. It didn't matter what was
designated as "home," but when you ran and got
there no one could touch you—you were safe!
God is "home." Proverbs 18:10 says, "The name
of the Lord is a strong tower; the righteous run
to it, and are safe." There's no doctor or medicine
or fallout shelter or secret service team—there is
NOTHING that can protect me like He can. And
there is no parent or spouse or child or friend who
cares for me like He does. I hear this when I read
John 15:13: "Greater love has no one than this: to
lay down one's life for one's friends." And I hear
this when I read the words of Jesus in Matthew
6:26: "Look at the birds of the air; they do not
sow or reap or store away in barns, and yet your
heavenly Father feeds them. Are you not much
more valuable than they?" Yes, He IS my fortress.
When "I walk through the valley of the shadow
of death" (Psalm 23:4 KJV), I have no reason to
be afraid, because He is with me, and He cares for
me and He is my fortress!

"I will not be shaken."

Well, duh—wouldn't that be foolish now that I
have finally heard what He told me in His Word!
No, I will NOT be shaken. Instead, I think I'll
take a nap.

It has been several years since I went on this search. At that
time, I was just writing for myself what I learned. I feel now,

however, an additional purpose was to save the truth for when you most needed it and were ready to listen.

Pause for

a Bird's-Eye View

If you are living in chaos, you may be feeling you have no control. It may seem you are a victim of your circumstances with no way out. Telling you that I found hope and rest based on what I read in the Bible may seem too simplistic and even ridiculous. Still, there were times I could hardly breathe due to the anxiety that weighed upon my chest, and I did find hope. I found the ability to rest, just like I told you. Please try not to judge too quickly. Treat what you read as a buffet. You don't eat everything at a buffet—some things you walk past. Stay with me. I believe you will find something within these pages you will want to choose, and it will nourish you.

Chapter 3

Change Requires Changes

Once, in a ladies Bible study, I met a Gwen. She was in her seventies and had spent most of her life trying to save her son. The son had a little girl, and Gwen had also taken on the responsibility of raising that child.

Gwen was a broken soul who cried as she shared with us her story of a lifetime of trying to save her son. The granddaughter, now a young adult, was making poor choices. Gwen said that instead of her granddaughter being grateful for the help she had given, she blamed her grandmother for everything wrong in her life.

Gwen's shoulders shook as she cried. She asked us to please pray for her loved ones. She said she had lost the will to get up each morning. It had taken all the effort she had that day to come to our study.

I was shocked a few weeks later, before our eight-week study was finished, when I received a call informing me Gwen had died. I'm not certain of the exact diagnosis, but I am sure her broken, hopeless heart held some responsibility.

The story of her tragic life and her sudden death impacted me. Gwen could no longer save anyone. Was she ever able? I was more committed than ever to learn what I needed to learn.

Change is not easy, but neither is remaining in a life of chaos.

Do you remember my counselor's remark at that first session, where he told me he didn't believe I could yet handle his advice about what to do? Well, the day finally came for him to tell me. He had been patient. Over the weeks, he had repeatedly heard me list my many burdens and sacrificial efforts to save my son, who was now twenty. The counselor also heard the list of progressively worse choices my son was making. I was still asking the same question: "How can I save my son?"

Perhaps the counselor detected a sense of urgency for the sake of my son. Perhaps the counselor thought, "Nothing else is working; so, I might as well tell her what I believe is best, ready or not." I'm not sure what he was thinking, but what he said was "You no longer need to allow your son to live in your home."

I now understand why the counselor thought I could not handle this advice on my first visit. After many weeks of sessions, I still couldn't handle it! I quickly responded, "Where would he go? He doesn't have a job. He would have more opportunity to be with the wrong people and make even more dangerous choices." Then, I shared my greatest fear: "He could die!"

The counselor calmly responded, "You're right. These things could happen, but it's the only chance he has to get better."

I left the counseling office that day without making another appointment. I went back to trying it my way. Then, two or three months later, I finally made another appointment. *My way still wasn't working!*

The situation at home had deteriorated. Now impersonating my child was this demanding, disrespectful, destructive stranger. To make matters even worse, my husband was pulling away. Home was no longer a refuge for him. He spent a lot of time at work, and even when he was home, we had little interaction. My marriage was in trouble! I felt alone. When I went back to the counselor, I said, "Tell me again—what do I need to do?"

I finally asked my son to leave. As I had feared, he did move into an undesirable location, and his drug usage progressed. Although he physically left my home, I did not let go. Like the weed in the poem "He Loved Too Strong," I continued to squeeze my son tightly. I called him often to check on him. I poured out my advice and criticism. I found him a job that he kept only a few weeks. When he told me he was out of food, I would take him bags of groceries.

I never let go, and I certainly never gave him to God. Sure, I'd pray and ask God to save my son, but then I'd take him back from God and try to save him myself. My son indeed had a problem, but so did I.

Finally, my last counseling session came, and it was one of the hardest moments of my life. Once again, the counselor listened as I whined about the same old problems and my same old efforts.

Dramatically, I told him that although I had really tried, I just could not be tough. I sniffed as I shared how I had recently allowed my son to come back home. I defended my decision by explaining how my son had told me he no longer had a place to stay and had not eaten since the previous morning. "He was so sweet and broken," I said to the counselor. "And he only asked to have a meal and spend one night."

Then, I shared how my son had remained that sweet, broken young man for less than twenty-four hours. The demanding, disrespectful, destructive stranger was quick to reappear and then refused to leave.

When I finally finished my story (and whining), the counselor spoke. This time, however, his response totally shocked me. "I understand it must be hard," he said. "The truth is most people never change. I have told you everything I can."

My mind did a spiral! "What?" I thought. "That's it?" After all this counseling, was he telling me I could not change? I left his office. Still running around my head were his words: "The truth is most people *never change.*"

I was depressed, but the depression did not last long. Then, I got mad. Finally, I remembered something from the Bible I had heard quoted. I picked up my Bible and searched until I found it. It was in Matthew 19:26: "Jesus looked at them and said, 'With man this is impossible, but with God all things are possible.'"

That's how it all started.

I decided right then and there that the counselor didn't know what he was talking about—I could change with God's help. I would change! My son's life depended upon it; my life depended upon it. I had found a valuable truth in God's recorded Word, and I was certain there were more to be found. I didn't make another counseling appointment, but I began to read, study, and meditate on the wisdom of the Creator. I was now determined. What do you think—did that counselor know telling me I couldn't change would have this effect on me?

Change is *not* easy. As a matter of fact, I'm sure the counselor spoke the truth when he said that most people never change. Some may not change because they are unaware they need to change. These people spend their lives blaming their circumstances on someone else. These people think, "If only *they* would change, then my life would be better." What such people don't realize is that they—themselves—can take control.

Others just don't know where to start. They are like a speeding train going in the wrong direction on the wrong track. How do they turn around?

Finally, there are some others who just aren't willing to put forth the effort.

Except for the last group, all can change.

I recently spoke with my youngest daughter. I shared with her what I just shared with you: the reasons why people do not change. She said, "Mom, there is another reason—sometimes people don't know they can change." She spoke about a dark period of her life when she was in an abusive relationship and battled depression. She said that at the time, she did not know there was a way to change. How sad that this precious child of mine did not understand that change was possible.

Once I had made the decision to change and learned that God's power was available, I immediately began to speak differently to my children. I started to speak words of hope and faith.

My daughter had to choose change on her own, but I do believe she may have begun to understand that change was possible when changes started happening in me.

Let's look at truths about change by examining a series of questions.

Self-Evident Truth

Matthew 19:26: "Jesus looked at them and said. 'With man this is impossible, but with God all things are possible.'"

Question 1 on Change:
Where Do You Find Wisdom?

There was much I needed to learn. By becoming wiser, I could be better prepared to interact or not interact (depending upon the situation) with those I loved. Of course, I must confess that my desire to change was still in hopes of saving others, more than for myself. But what a worthy by-product!

Early in my journey for wisdom, I found a particular verse from Proverbs in the Bible; and I recalled it often.

Self-Evident Truth

Proverbs 15:22 "Plans fail for lack of counsel, but with many advisors they succeed."

If you turn on the television or pick up a magazine, you can find many who are ready to give you advice. But I wasn't just looking for counsel; I was looking for wise counsel. If I sought a book, I looked to see who recommended it. Did they agree with truths I found to be self-evident? If I was accessing someone's advice by reading an article, watching a television program, listening to a radio program, or sitting down with a person one on one, I wanted to know if their truths aligned with the Creator's. I would ask myself, "Where did they obtain their knowledge?" I wasn't seeking opinions or the latest new idea; I was seeking wisdom!

In looking back at my counseling experiences, I recognize that I never found a Fort Knox of wisdom. The wisdom I gained was more like a bunch of nuggets I accumulated along the way.

There was just the one counselor with whom I met over an extended period of time. After all of those hours of sessions with him, I could condense what I learned into three simple propositions, but what a powerful three:

1) Sometimes the best way to help our children is to stop helping our children;
2) Change is not easy; so, most people don't change; and
3) I am worth saving, too!

Looking back, I'm sure he repeated the same things to me in various ways, always with hopes my ears would finally hear what he was saying. I am grateful for his willingness to be persistent and sometimes tough with me because that's what eventually opened up my hearing. I know, too, that he was not just trying to help me; he was also trying to help my son.

Many of the nuggets of wisdom along the way came from people I met only in passing. There was a caseworker at the drug rehabilitation center my son attended in his late teens. She conked me in the head one day with one of the nuggets. She had listened to me pour out my heart about my poor son and his struggles. She heard me place the blame on others, including myself, for his wrong choices. Then, I proceeded to throw my husband under the bus, as I labeled him unsupportive and unsympathetic. I confided how recently my husband had even had the audacity to suggest we move away and leave my son behind. I reassured her that I was dedicated to helping my son and would never leave him. In fact, I said that I would leave my husband before that would happen.

That's when she spoke (and threw the nugget): "Well, if you left your husband for that boy in there, then you'd be sicker than he is! You don't need to worry about your son. If you left, he'd find some young thing that would want to save him." (She had already seen a girlfriend coming by for visits.) She continued, "He's not going to get better until he runs out of women trying to save him."

This two-week program, followed by several months of outpatient visits and group therapy sessions, caused a stress on our finances. However, this caseworker's wisdom may have been the most valuable nugget from the experience. Although her truth fell on deaf ears that day, I eventually recalled her words at a time when I was able to recognize wisdom.

Other nuggets came from a counselor, Mr. Dave, who met with my son off and on from my son's late teens to early adulthood. My son liked Mr. Dave. I can recall three different nuggets this counselor whirled at me. The first one was when I called him after my son had been seeing him for a few months. I said I was really worried and concerned because my son seemed to be getting worse, not better. Mr. Dave firmly said, "Let me tell you something. Why don't you try not getting too excited when it looks like things are getting better and not get too upset when things don't look so good? Change takes time, but as long as your son is alive, you keep having hope. He might not even change in your lifetime, but you always keep hoping. If you're going to have an active imagination, use it to picture good things happening!"

The second nugget he threw at me was when I called to set up an appointment for my son after he had not had counseling for several weeks. I thought Mr. Dave would be happy about this. I was wrong. He asked me, "Why didn't your son call to make the appointment?"

I said I didn't know, but that I was so glad my son was willing to go that I didn't question his asking me to do it. Wrong answer!

Mr. Dave said through gritted teeth, at least that's how I heard it, "Every time you do something for your son that he should be able to do on his own, it's like telling him you don't believe he's capable of doing it, that you don't have any faith in him." I didn't like hearing that at the time, but I needed to hear it.

Finally, the last nugget (or perhaps this one was more of a confirmation) was when my husband and I finally did decide to make a move out of state. My son was twenty-one years old. I called Mr. Dave and told him we were moving and that I didn't know where my son would be staying. I told Mr. Dave I wanted to let him know because he might be hearing from my son. Mr. Dave laughed out loud. (I'd never heard him laugh or even sound happy before.) He said, "That's wonderful news! Now, maybe that young man can get better!" Yes, Mr. Dave tended to hit me between the eyes with his nuggets, but perhaps he knew that was the only way to get me to consider them.

I attended quite a few group therapy sessions, and I am sure there was wisdom there (many have been helped through group programs); but I'm afraid I missed out on most of that benefit. I did find it is true that misery loves company, because I found comfort in knowing I wasn't the only daughter or parent of an alcohol or drug abuser. I also met individuals who had learned to find joy and peace in the middle of chaos. Perhaps some of them, like me, had learned how this was possible through the guidance of the Creator and His truths.

Baskets of wisdom nuggets came from some very special friends. Soon after we were married, my husband and I had developed a very close friendship with a couple, Charlie and Judy. Charlie coincidentally (or perhaps by divine placement) was a professional counselor, specializing in substance abuse and marriage counseling. At the time we met them, we had no idea how much we would need counsel in both of those areas—or how this precious couple would be willing to invest their time and love into us. They listened; they offered wisdom. I'm not sure Larry and I would be together today if not for this couple's patient love and wise counsel.

Not only did Charlie help us work through trials in our marriage, but also he and his business partner, Byron (another divinely placed close friend), poured themselves into the life of our son. There is a bond and love between these men and our son that will last forever. What are the odds of moving into a town and making new friendships with two men with such credentials and wisdom in the *exact* area my husband, my son, and I needed *when* we needed it? Could the Creator have arranged these meetings? We display their gift of nuggets on the mantles of our hearts.

My ears were now open to a bounty of wisdom, most of which I found in the Bible.

Next I present some of those key concepts, along with my thoughts.

Self-Evident Truths

Proverbs 19:20: "Listen to advice and accept discipline, and at the end you will be counted among the wise."

Lesson: Perhaps I had made my mistakes, but it was not too late to get smarter and get it right.

———❦———

Proverbs 20:18: "Plans are established by seeking advice; so if you wage war, obtain guidance."

Lesson: I remind you of an earlier truth: the Enemy exists. Make no mistake; this is war! Get help!

———❦———

Psalm 16:7: "I will praise the LORD, who counsels me; even at night my heart instructs me."

Lesson: There is no better counselor than the Creator.

———❦———

Psalm 32:8: "I will instruct you and teach you in the way you should go; I will counsel you with my loving eye on you."

Lesson: *There has never been a better counselor, and there never will be a better, more loving Counselor.*

In John 14, Jesus was talking to His disciples about His upcoming return to heaven. Once He had died on the cross as a sacrifice for our sins and had been resurrected, fulfilling the old prophecies, His mission on earth would be complete. He would be returning to heaven to prepare a place for those who believed in Him and accepted Him as their Savior. He told the disciples that they would not be alone—the Spirit of God, the Holy Spirit, would come to live in them. The Holy Spirit would be their help and give them counsel!

I find this truth about the Counselor to be self-evident:

> And I will ask the Father, and he will give you another advocate to help you and be with you forever—the Spirit of truth. The world cannot accept him, because it neither sees him nor knows him. But you know him, for he lives with you and will be in you. (John 14:16–17)

Those of us who believe have access to the ultimate Counselor every minute of every day.

Finally, as we end this discussion about seeking wisdom, I'd like to close with a truth that further emphasizes the Holy Spirit's role as our ultimate Counselor and reveals why I have such a desire to help you.

Self-Evident Truth

2 Corinthians 1:3–4: "Praise be to the God and Father of our Lord Jesus Christ, the Father of compassion and the God of all comfort, who

comforts us in all our troubles, so that we can
comfort those in any trouble with the comfort we
ourselves receive from God."

Yes, He has helped me through so much. My hope is that you,
too, will find comfort within these pages and from the Comforter
Himself!

Question 2 on Change: What's on Your Mind?

The bookstores are full of books about the secrets of
success. I've read many of them. I have watched many television
interviews of highly successful people. I've also attended
seminars on how to be successful in business. One point I
repeatedly heard stressed was the importance of what was in
your heart and on your mind. You have to want something bad
enough! You have to believe you can achieve! You have to have
faith (see it before you see it)! Finally, you also have to guard
against the thoughts that work against the end result you desire!
Does all this emphasis on our thoughts align with God's Word?
We will examine that here.

When Mr. Dave was reprimanding me for my negative
imagination, he could have simply asked me, "What's on your
mind?" However, he didn't have to ask because he knew—it was
coming out of my mouth.

For me, negative thinking had been a lifelong habit. I'm not
sure I was even aware of my negativity. I often quoted positive
sayings. I would even have described myself as a positive thinker.
There was, however, a battle going on inside my heart and mind.
I worried. I could not see past the negative circumstances around
me. At times, I would even start crying as I played out my greatest
fears in my mind. I thought my negative thoughts were a logical

consequence of the negative situations in my life. But Mr. Dave suggested I had a choice.

I finally turned to the words of the Creator to see if He agreed with Mr. Dave.

Self-Evident Truth

> **Philippians 4:8:** "Finally, brothers and sisters, whatever is true, whatever is noble, whatever is right, whatever is pure, whatever is lovely, whatever is admirable—if anything is excellent or praiseworthy—think about such things."

The verse above became the gauge for my thoughts. At first this was exhausting, because it seemed dark thoughts were continually running across my mind. I decided to write out a positive affirmation about what I wanted my life to be; I read it often. Then, I memorized verses from the Word of the Creator, like Philippians 4:8; and I would quote them if my thoughts turned in a negative direction.

I began to guard against listening to negative things, which sometimes meant avoiding certain people in my life. I chose to listen to positive music. Sometimes I would sing happy, uplifting songs out loud to drive away the clouds of negativity.

The Bible became my, well, "bible." I found within its pages words of hope and help and promise. I often read from the book of Psalms—for example, Psalm 121, which reminded me that I wasn't alone and that I had help.

My smile became brighter, more sincere. I started expecting challenges to work out. I started trusting the Creator to give me the help I needed to face the tough times.

I believe that taking control of my thoughts was the most important change of my life.

Self-Evident Truths

Proverbs 4:23: "Above all else, guard your heart, for everything you do flows from it."

Lesson: Everything we do in our lives begins with our thoughts. If we want a better life, we start with better thoughts.

Luke 6:45: "A good man brings good things out of the good stored up in his heart, and an evil man brings evil things out of the evil stored up in his heart. For the mouth speaks what the heart is full of."

Lesson: There is a relationship between the thoughts we think and the words we speak. This verse tells us that our words reflect our thoughts. I also believe our words can help to change our thoughts.

Psalm 139:23–24: "Search me, God, and know my heart; test me and know my anxious thoughts. See if there is any offensive way in me, and lead me in the way everlasting."

Lesson: God will help us if we ask Him.

Question 3 on Change: What Are You Saying?

In reviewing my life, I noticed that my sins and mistakes were often intertwined with the words I spoke. There were times I spoke in anger. There were times I should have remained silent but selfishly chose to be heard. There were times I spoke without thinking. I'm a talker and may have used more than my share of words in my life. Some of them hurt others.

I also hurt myself with negative words I sent in my own direction. Not only does the mouth speak what the heart is full of, as we read in Luke 6:45, but also the heart (or mind) hears what your own mouth is saying. As I talked about my greatest fears and my "hopeless" circumstances, who was listening? *I* was listening. I listen and take into my thoughts *all* that I hear, but I hear no one louder than I hear *myself*. How can I live a life of victory if I continually hear myself predict gloom and doom? Beyond the negative impact on my life, how do my words and actions of hopelessness affect my loved ones?

What does the Creator have to say about our words?

Self-Evident Truths

Proverbs 21:23: "Those who guard their mouths and their tongues keep themselves from calamity."

James 3:6: "The tongue also is a fire, a world of evil among the parts of the body. It corrupts the whole body, sets the whole course of one's life on fire, and is itself set on fire by hell."

Proverbs 18:21: "The tongue has power of life and death, and those who love it will eat its fruit."

The Creator makes it clear that our words are important and have the power of life and death. I finally realized that if I wanted to make a change in my life, I needed to change the words coming out of my own mouth; I needed to choose to speak life.

The following truths provide lessons for life-producing words:

Self-Evident Truths

Ephesians 4:29: "Do not let any unwholesome talk come out of your mouths, but only what is helpful for building others up according to their needs, that it may benefit those who listen."

Lesson: Taking control of your tongue may not be easy, but it is important.

Psalm 19:14: "May these words of my mouth and this meditation of my heart be pleasing in your sight, LORD, my Rock and my Redeemer."

Lesson: As always, we have help!

As I began to guard my words more carefully, I was amazed how quickly I saw the change in my family and myself. My confidence grew, and my hope was renewed. Soon I was not only speaking words of faith, but also I was starting to believe answers were coming. My loved ones heard the change. They, too, began to express hope. My words were producing life; I was seeing the fruit!

Question 4 on Change: Why Does It Take Manure to Grow Things?

As we began to turn our train around and get onto the right track, my husband and I discovered new interests. One of our new hobbies became planting flowers and watching them grow. Actually, I was the one who first expressed an interest in flowers. Then Larry, who grew up on a farm, quickly recognized my lack of understanding about the basics of gardening and joined me. My plants weren't growing. I had been careful to plant the shade plants in the shade and the sunshine-loving plants in the sun. I had watered my flowers each morning. Still, my plants were puny, had few blossoms, and were starting to die.

One day, Larry met me in the backyard with a bag of manure and said, "This ground needs some nutrients. Manure will make these plants grow." He was right—our backyard became a beautiful explosion of color!

Manure can be dangerous. Piles of it can produce heat and methane gas, which can lead to spontaneous combustions and fire (sometimes major explosions). Manure can also contaminate water, attract insects, cause diseases, and it stinks! On the other hand, however, Larry was right—it can produce growth.

Manure has value; "manure times" have value, too!

Wikipedia's Definition of Manure

"Manure is organic matter used as organic fertilizer in agriculture. Manure contributes to the fertility of the soil by adding organic matter and nutrients, such as nitrogen, that are trapped by bacteria in the soil. Higher organisms then feed on the fungi and bacteria in a chain of life that comprises the soil food web. It is also a product obtained after decomposition of organic matter like cow-dung, which replenishes the soil with essential elements and adds humus to the soil."

Life can have its share of manure. We can call them tough times, times in the valleys of life, trials, etc. I personally think *manure times* is a good term to describe these times—they can stink but needed growth can come from them.

One of the major changes in my life was to recognize the value of the manure times. Let's pause to see what the Creator says about them; however, the Creator didn't actually use the word manure. (Hopefully, He's not shaking His head at my word choice.)

Self-Evident Truths

James 1:2–4: "Consider it pure joy, my brothers and sisters, whenever you face trials of many kinds, because you know that the testing of your faith produces perseverance. Let perseverance finish its work so that you may be mature and complete, not lacking anything."

Romans 5:3–4: "Not only so, but we also glory in our sufferings, because we know that suffering produces perseverance; perseverance, character; and character, hope."

Over the years, was I too quick to try to help my children before they were able to learn a valuable lesson? Did I ever protect them from the consequences of their actions in order to keep life's manure away? Unknowingly and in the name of love, did I sometimes withhold a life-giving by-product of their actions? Did I ever prevent the opportunity for my loved ones to develop perseverance, character, maturity, and hope? Even if my answer (or yours) to any of these questions is yes, the past cannot be changed. We can, however, choose to change our actions from this day forward.

I recall once when my son told someone, "My mom is like Super Mom!" He went on to share how I never stopped working and I was always there giving of myself and helping him and others. "She never gets tired," he added. At the time, I enjoyed the praise, maybe even had a need for this praise, but in truth, I *was* tired!

Now, however, I understand that the greatest compliment to a parent is to have raised children to a level of maturity where they do not need their parents. Instead, those daughters and sons look within themselves and to God for answers. They should love and respect their parents—yes, absolutely. Perhaps they can turn to their parents for a bit of wisdom on occasion—no problem. But to *need* their parents' help in their day-to-day lives—not good. This kind of need is not a compliment but is instead a warning that there's not been enough manure provided so that it could do its good work.

I should add that it was the manure times in my life that gave me the courage and strength to endure the pain of change. Change wasn't easy; change took time. But I had the perseverance to endure. I traded my Super Mom cape for gardening gloves. Having learned the value of manure, I was rewarded with time to sit in the backyard and watch the flowers grow.

I Walked a Mile with Pleasure

I walked a mile with Pleasure;
She chatted all the way;
But I never learned a thing from her
For all she had to say.

I walked a mile with Sorrow,
And never a word said she;
But, oh! The things I learned from her
When Sorrow walked with me.

—Robert Browning Hamilton

Chapter 4

The Search for Answers Continues

For years, fear was the ever-present emotion that controlled my life. Anxiety attacks were so common that I ignored them and kept going. Restless sleep was my norm. As I shared earlier, rest was hard to find, because fear was rarely quiet.

Fear Is a Foe

During that first visit with the counselor, as I related the feeling that I was watching my son drown, it was the voice of fear that spoke from me. This emotion was consuming my life and was actually affecting me physically.

Finally, I decided to see what the Creator's Word had to say about this powerful foe. What I learned empowered me.

Self-Evident Truths

Isaiah 41:10: "So do not fear, for I am with you; do not be dismayed, for I am your God. I will strengthen you and help you; I will uphold you with my righteous right hand."

Lesson: Help is available.

Joshua 1:9: "Have I not commanded you? Be strong and courageous. Do not be afraid; do not be discouraged, for the LORD your God will be with you wherever you go."

Lesson: We are not supposed to be afraid.

Deuteronomy 31:8: "The LORD himself goes before you and will be with you; he will never leave you nor forsake you. Do not be afraid; do not be discouraged."

Lesson: When we have God, we are never alone.

John 14:27: "Peace I leave with you; my peace I give you. I do not give to you as the world gives. Do not let your hearts be troubled and do not be afraid."

Lesson: *We have a choice: peace or fear.*

What are your stories that evoke fear? Do they include words such as drugs, addiction, homeless, anger, jail, and violence? Mine do. Instead of those stories, let us choose to focus, for now, on a story that can give us the strength and knowledge to overcome.

When I examined the story in Luke 8:22–25 about Jesus and the disciples crossing the lake, I came face to face with a truth I had been missing. As they were crossing the lake and Jesus was napping, a fierce storm came down on the lake. Verse 24 says, "The disciples went and woke him, saying, 'Master, Master, we're going to drown!' He got up and rebuked the wind and the raging waters; the storm subsided, and all was calm."

What Jesus said then to the disciples is what shook me. In verse 25, Jesus asks, "Where is your faith?" Jesus told them (and me) that responding in fear is a choice; and it is not responding with faith. I think that's where our journey is taking us; let's learn the truth about faith. Before we go there, please read the following verses and self-evident truths which further emphasize that victory over fear is available. By the end of the verses, you will find the answer to driving out fear. We will refer back to these verses at the end of our look at faith.

Self-Evident Truths

1 John 4:15–18: "If anyone acknowledges that Jesus is the Son of God, God lives in them and they in God. And so we know and rely on the love God has for us. God is love. Whoever lives in love lives in God, and God in them. This is how love is made complete among us so that we will have confidence on the day of judgment: In this world we are like Jesus. There is no fear in love. But perfect love drives out fear, because fear has to do with punishment. The one who fears is not made perfect in love."

Lesson: God's love is perfect; perfect love drives out fear.

John 14:1–4 (NKJV): "Let not your heart be troubled; you believe in God, believe also in Me. In My Father's house are many mansions; if *it were* not *so*, I would have told you. I go to prepare a place for you. And if I go and prepare a place for you, I will come again and receive you to Myself; that where I am, *there* you may be also. And where I go you know, and the way you know."

Lesson: The future can be bright!

23rd Psalm (KJV)

The Lord is my shepherd;
I shall not want.
He maketh me to lie down in green pastures:
He leadeth me beside the still waters.
He restoreth my soul:
He leadeth me in the paths of righteousness for his name's sake.
Yea, though I walk through the valley of the shadow of death,
I will fear no evil:
For thou art with me;
Thy rod and thy staff they comfort me.
Thou preparest a table before me in the presence of mine enemies:
Thou anointest my head with oil;
My cup runneth over.
Surely goodness and mercy shall follow me all the days of my life:
And I will dwell in the house of the LORD for ever.

Faith: See It Before You See It

In bookstores, you can find shelves of positive-thinking books that teach on visualizing your goals. Long before I realized the answers to my life's questions were written in one book, the Bible, I read many of these other books and even attended several business seminars that taught this principle. At one such seminar, the speaker said, "If you don't see it before you ever see it, you'll never see it." He talked about writing down your goals and posting pictures of your dreams around you to motivate your efforts. Perhaps he had read the Creator's book and the best definition I've ever seen on faith:

> Now faith is confidence in what we hope for and assurance about what we do not see. (Hebrews 11:1)

How can you see peace in the middle of a battle? How can you see victory when devastation surrounds you? When crisis after crisis is in front of your face blocking your view, how do you see your loved one living out the good plan designed by the Creator? Furthermore, God says in the above verse that we can *confidently* see what we hope for. If you could watch a video of the future, showing how everything works out beyond your wildest imagination, would it not be easier to have peace and rest? Of course it would. Faith can be a "video" you choose to play in your mind and heart if you believe and trust in God. We can choose to see it before we see it. When, we do, the results are powerful!

Over the years, I certainly had a wild imagination, but it was wildly negative. I shared with you before how Mr. Dave chastised me for using my negative imagination when thinking about my son. After I had described to Mr. Dave my fears of the possible negatives that could happen, he told me I should use my active imagination to generate pictures of a good future for my son. Mr.

Dave knew that fear is a foe. It is also the opposite of faith. Both can have powerful results, but only with faith will you get the results your heart desires.

Faith is the key we are given by God to unlock the treasures He has for us. This proposition is not a mystical secret—it is revealed in His Word. Chapter 11 of Hebrews, for example, is like a *Who's Who of Proven Faith with Amazing Results*. In this chapter, God tells us in the first verse what faith is, and then God goes on to emphasize its importance. After that, He gives us the Who's Who list: "By faith Abel ... By faith Enoch ... By faith Noah ... By faith Abraham ... By faith Isaac ... By faith Jacob ... By faith Joseph ... By faith Moses ..." More are mentioned after that.

The stories are there to remind us of what God has done in the past when those who believed in Him had faith. One reads in verse 7 that by faith Noah saved his family. Verses 8 and 9 tell how "by faith Abraham ... made his home in the promised land ... as did Isaac and Jacob, who were heirs with him of the same promise...." And verse 12 tells how by faith the aged Abraham, who was "as good as dead" when it came to having children, nonetheless "became a father with descendants as numerous as the stars in the sky and as countless as the sand on the seashore ..." Furthermore, we are told in verse 11 that Sarah, who was past her childbearing age, gave birth to Isaac "because she considered him faithful who had made the promise."

> By faith the people passed through the Red Sea as on dry land; ... (Hebrews 11:29)
>
> By faith the walls of Jericho fell, ... (Hebrews 11:30)
>
> By faith Abraham, when God tested him, offered Isaac as a sacrifice. He who had embraced the

promises was about to sacrifice his one and only son, even though God had said to him, "It is through Isaac that your offspring will be reckoned." Abraham reasoned that God could even raise the dead, and so in a manner of speaking he did receive Isaac back from death. (Hebrews 11:17–19)

The heroes of Hebrews 11 and other examples of faith in the Bible teach me about faith; they also remind me to continually think about what God has done for others when they came to Him in faith. When I am faced with a gigantic problem in my life, it can be reassuring to remember a shepherd boy named David who brought down his giant with God's help (1 Samuel 17). When I am tempted to worry about my children, it is encouraging to remember that Noah's faith saved his family.

I love a story told in Matthew 15 about a mother who goes to Jesus and persistently pleads for Him to save her daughter. Jesus answers, "Woman, you have great faith. Your request is granted." The Bible tells us, "And her daughter was healed that very hour." It is comforting to hear that a *mother's faith saved her child*. That verse makes me say *wow*; and wow verses are everywhere in the Bible.

Over the years, the more I read these stories the better was my visualizing that allowed me to have *confidence* in what I *hoped for* and the *assurance* about what I *did not see*.

The following verses lead us to our most important pause for a bird's eye view. These additional truths of the Creator further emphasize the power of faith.

Self-Evident Truths

Matthew 17:20: "He replied, 'Because you have so little faith. Truly I tell you, if you have faith as small as a mustard seed, you can say to this mountain, "Move from here to there," and it will move. Nothing will be impossible for you.'"

Luke 7:50: "Jesus said to the woman, 'Your faith has saved you; go in peace.'"

Luke 17:19: "Then he said to him, 'Rise and go; your faith has made you well.'"

Pause for

a Bird's-Eye View

Before I shared the first word in this collection of stories and lessons, I thought of you, and that has not changed. Do you cry yourself to sleep out of fear for your loved one? Do you find it hard to sleep at all? Does your life feel hopeless? Are you spinning plates trying to save your loved ones?

More than anything, I wonder, "Do you know Jesus?" If you do, I at least know you have a place to turn—to a friend who loves you, to a Creator who has left you His Word to guide you. I hope you are finding comfort as you are reminded He will help you.

Perhaps, however, you are like I was most of my life. I knew Jesus, but I lived my life as if solving all of life's problems was up to me. I went to church on most Sundays, but I rarely read God's Word. I would occasionally pray, but I lived unaware of His love and His nearness. Help was readily available, but I foolishly chose to struggle alone. If this is you, I hope I have reminded you to turn your eyes to Him.

Finally, if you are someone who does not know Jesus, you are especially on my mind. Maybe you have heard of Him, but you did not comprehend that He is alive and knows you and loves you—always has, always will. Did you know He wants you to believe in Him so He can help you? God does not force Himself on us. We are given the choice to believe in Him and His Son Jesus or to choose the sin of the world and an eternity separated from Him. When we choose to believe in God's Son, by faith, we become His children and can ask Him to help us. When we choose not to accept Him, not to have faith, we do not have access to His power, and we choose to battle alone in our lives.

Self-Evident Truths

Romans 3:23: "for all have sinned, and fall short of the glory of God,"

Romans 10:17: "Consequently, faith comes from hearing the message, and the message is heard through the word about Christ."

John 3:16: "For God so loved the world that he gave his one and only Son, that whoever believes in him shall not perish but have eternal life."

Ephesians 2:8: "For it is by grace you have been saved, through faith—and this is not from yourselves, it is the gift of God-"

Romans 10:10: "For it is with your heart that you believe and are justified, and it is with your mouth that you profess your faith and are saved."

I was just a child when I heard about Jesus, but something inside of me *knew* it was true—that was faith. I couldn't see Him, but I *knew.* I prayed a prayer telling God I did believe in Jesus and knew He was God's Son. I asked God to forgive me, a sinner. I chose Him. I remember being so happy to have prayed that prayer. I wish I had understood the fullness of what I had done: I was at that moment a child of God. I had been born again so as to live eternally with the Spirit of God in me. From that point onward, in faith, I could take all my troubles to Him and He would help me. Most of my life's tears could have been avoided had I understood the whole truth.

In the next chapter, we will look at the power of prayer and God's presence in our lives once we have chosen Him. At the end of that chapter, there is a prayer I have written in case you would like to be led into accepting Jesus as your Lord and Savior. You may choose to word your prayer in the way your heart leads you. If you want to jump a few pages ahead and do that now, go ahead, but be sure and come back and read the pages you passed. You don't want to miss the whole truth like I did.

As we close this chapter, consider a Bible passage with another truth that I find to be self-evident. (We read some of these verses before, but they are worth rereading at this moment.)

Self-Evident Truth

1 John 4:7–16: "Dear friends, let us love one another, for love comes from God. Everyone who loves has been born of God and knows God. Whoever does not love does not know God, because God is love. This is how God showed his love among us: He sent his one and only son into the world that we might live through him. This is love: not that we loved God, but that he loved us and sent his son as an atoning sacrifice for our sins. Dear friends, since God so loved us, we also ought to love one another. No one has ever seen God; but if we love one another, God lives in us and his love is made complete in us. This is how we know that we live in him and he in us: He has given us his Spirit. And we have seen and testify that the Father has sent his Son to be the Savior of the world. If anyone acknowledges that Jesus is the Son of God, God lives in them and they in God. And so we know and rely on the love God has for us. God is love. Whoever lives in love lives in God, and God in them."

The Choice

Door Number One;
Door Number Two—
He stood on the stage
Trying to choose.

The curtains were open,
So he could see
The prizes behind
That he could receive.

Behind the first
Was glitter and gold,
More gidgets and gadgets
To use and to hold.

Behind Number Two
Was simply a cross.
"To choose it," he thought,
"Would surely be loss."

"Wait," said the host,
"Don't choose with zest—
What looks to be better
May not really be best."

With closer inspection,
Behind Number One
He found smoke and mirrors,
And he'd only begun.

The gidgets and gadgets
Were starting to rust,
And the glitter and gold—
They merely were dust.

Then, he turned
To Door Number Two.
With an old wooden cross,
What could he do?

But as he looked closer
He found at the cross
Abundance of treasure
Instead of a loss.

A lifetime supply
Of mercy and love,
Plus, the joy and peace
He'd been dreaming of.

With the cross
Came a mansion, too,
And a vacation in Paradise
All eternity through.

Of course you know
He chose Number Two.
But this game is no game—
Which life do you choose?

—Ricki Elks

Chapter 5

Prayer, Praise, Presence, and Power

In my earliest memory of myself praying, I am hiding under my bed covers, being so afraid of the dark. I guess that I was about five or six years old. Although I had never seen my parents pray, I had learned about prayer. On some Sundays, my friend and his mother, our next-door neighbors, would invite me to walk with them the few blocks to a local church. It was there I heard about Jesus. I heard how much He loved me and how He could hear and answer my prayers.

I remember promising God, on many dark nights, that if He would keep me safe, I would be good. Then, to help God out, I would arrange my covers in a pile at the end of my bed and sleep under them. I felt certain that if someone or something came into my room, they or it would think no one was there. Ironically, I spent much of my adult life with same idea of God and prayer—it was comforting to take my troubles to Him, but I would then pick them back up, along with my fears, and proceed to attempt to solve my own problems. If only I had turned to the best resource for answers, God's Word, I would have understood He did not want my help, only my faith.

There are many ways to pray and different kinds of prayers. Some people simply bow their head and pray, while others choose to get on their knees and bow. Some like to walk around while they talk to God. I have prayed all of these ways, but I have also prayed while driving, doing laundry, or working in the yard. Often, I choose to write out my prayers in a journal. At times my prayers are just a conversation with my friend who is with me. I may simply be telling Him how wonderful I know Him to be, and how much I trust Him. Other times, my prayers express to Him my thankfulness. He has given me so much, helped me through lots of tough times, and answered so many prayers—I just want to tell Him how thankful I am. Then, there are times my prayers are cries for help, and believe me—I have cried out to Him many, many times.

I recently pulled out some old prayer journals. I thought I'd share with you pieces of some past conversations I've had with the Creator and my current reflections about them.

July 24, 1990
… Lord, here I am. I need You totally. I do not have the answers or the power I need in this world. As a wife, mother, friend, and Christian, I do need Your guidance. I pray to be better at loving You and trusting You …

Reflection: At least I knew then that He had the answers. He has taken me to a place where I love and trust Him more, but the journey wasn't always easy.

September 29, 1990
Dear Lord, I have always heard people talk about having a personal relationship with Jesus. Writing to You makes it feel more personal, but I pray that more and more I learn to listen to You and allow You to be my friend.

Reflection: I have learned to listen, and He is my friend.

April 26, 1993
My Dearest Lord, my problems feel like giants, but giants are insignificant to You. I give all my giants to You. I'm sorry that I have waited until I got this many giants—so many that I knew I couldn't handle alone. I should have been giving them to You all along. Thank you for sending Charles and Judy to me—it is good, so good to have a friendship with someone who loves You ...

Reflection: It sounds like I was starting to learn some things, but I had much more to learn. Also, I had been praying for God to put someone in my life who loved Him and would tell me some things I needed to hear. Charles was a marriage counselor. He had also been a drug and alcohol counselor for many years. He was a friend and counselor to our son. He and his wife, Judy, gave hours of wise counsel to my husband and me over the years. New friends with marriage and drug and alcohol counseling experience—only God could have orchestrated that divine introduction!

August 22, 1994
Dearest Lord, I cry out to You to save my Daddy ...

Reflection: Eight years after I wrote this prayer, my dad accepted Jesus as his Lord and Savior. After sixty years of being addicted to alcohol, my dad stopped drinking. Prayers are not always answered instantly, but God is listening.

April 24, 2002

Dear Lord, I need You—I am crying out to You! Please help me ...

June 26, 2002
Lord, only You know our hearts. Only You know our pain. Only You have the answer. Only You know how badly we need You.

September 3, 2002
Father, we need You. I give to you this night—the pain in this house, the anger, the fear ... Please touch all of us in this house.

September 9, 2002
Dearest Lord, what's wrong with me? Please help me with my relationships with my children. If only I can learn to let them go and give them to You ...

Reflection: He finally got my attention. I finally listened to Him in His Word.

July 27, 2004
Father, I pray You will open Joshua's eyes and heart, so he can see your love and your Truth. I claim in the Name of Jesus—Joshua is a man of God, a good husband, a good father, a good son, and a good testimony of the power of God. I claim Joshua to be honest, faithful with good works and a good heart. Lord, I pray and claim he will follow your perfect will for his life. Thank you, Amen.

Reflection: This was a prayer of faith. I know God heard it. God is still working on my son (and me); but it is amazing how much of this prayer is true today.

November 1, 2004
Father, HELP PLEASE! Please, please, please, please Help. I cry out to You, Father ... I do not have the answers, but You have them.

April 28, 2012
Father, here I am on this plane flying toward home. Joshua graduates in two weeks from Teen Challenge. You put him in a place that has allowed him to be filled with Your wisdom and love. You put people in his life that love You and him. You answered my prayers ...

Reflection: Yes, God listens and answers prayers.

There are some missing journals. They may be in boxes in the attic or may have been accidentally thrown away in one of at least a half dozen moves we made since I started the first prayer journal about twenty-six years ago. Also, there are journal gaps from some time periods when I didn't write down my prayers.

Journaling, however, has allowed me to clearly see God working in my life, sometimes even in small ways that I might have otherwise missed. It has also made me realize that it is not unusual to wait to see our prayers answered—sometimes we may wait years.

In our prayers and praise to God in the name of Jesus and with faith, the Holy Spirit of God is present, and there is power!

Self-Evident Truths

Philippians 4:6: "Do not be anxious about anything, but in every situation, by prayer and petition, with thanksgiving, present your requests to God."

Matthew 21:22: "If you believe, you will receive whatever you ask for in prayer."

John 14:26–27: "But the Advocate, the Holy Spirit, whom the Father will send in my name, will teach you all things and will remind you of everything I have said to you. Peace I leave with you; my peace I give you. I do not give to you as the world gives. Do not let your hearts be troubled and do not be afraid."

James 5:13: "Is anyone among you in trouble? Let them pray. Is anyone happy? Let them sing songs of praise."

2 Timothy 1:7: "For the Spirit God gave us does not make us timid, but gives us power, love and self-discipline."

John 14:13–14: "And I will do whatever you ask in my name, so that the Father may be glorified in the Son. You may ask me for anything in my name, and I will do it."

Matthew 6 tells us about one day when Jesus had finished praying, and the disciples asked Him to teach them how to pray. This is how Jesus answered them:

This, then, is how you should pray:

Our Father in heaven,
hallowed be your name,
your kingdom come,

your will be done,
on earth as it is in heaven.
Give us today our daily bread.
And forgive us our debts,
as we also have forgiven our debtors.
And lead us not into temptation,
but deliver us from the evil one. (Matthew 6:9–13)

The prayer that Jesus, Himself, gives us has praise and power. He also teaches us to go to the Father with our needs to receive help.

The gospel of Luke describes an example Jesus gave the disciples to show them an additional truth about prayer. See what Jesus shared.

Then Jesus said to them, "Suppose you have a friend, and you go to him at midnight and say, 'Friend, lend me three loaves of bread; a friend of mine on a journey has come to me, and I have no food to offer him.' And suppose the one inside answers, 'Don't bother me. The door is already locked, and my children and I are in bed. I can't get up and give you anything.' I tell you, even though he will not get up and give you the bread because of friendship, yet because of your shameless audacity he will surely get up and give you as much as you need." (Luke 11:5–8)

So, there we have it straight from the mouth of Jesus. If we don't see our prayers answered, we need to keep on knocking, keep on praying, until we see before us that which our heart desires and for which we have believed. Jesus has certainly seen my shameless audacity, because I have knocked for years to see some prayers answered; for others, I am still knocking.

Jesus sums up in the ninth verse what we should do:

> So I say to you: Ask and it will be given to you;
> seek and you will find; knock and the door
> will be opened to you. For everyone who asks
> receives; the one who seeks finds; and to the one
> who knocks, the door will be opened. (Luke
> 11:9–10)

These words that the Holy Spirit inspired in the book of
Ephesians are also my prayer for you:

> I pray that the eyes of your heart may be
> enlightened in order that you may know the
> hope to which he has called you, the riches of
> his glorious inheritance in his holy people, and
> his incomparably great power for us who believe.
> That power is the same as the mighty strength
> he exerted when he raised Christ from the dead
> and seated him at his right hand in the heavenly
> realms, far above all rule and authority, power
> and dominion, and every name that is invoked,
> not only in the present age but also in the one to
> come. (Ephesians 1:18–21)

Our Creator, who made heaven and earth, is waiting for you
to choose Him!

Pause for

a Bird's-Eye View
That Can Change Your Life
and Your Eternity!

From our self-evident truths, we have learned that we all are born into sin. We have learned the truth that Jesus is the Son of God. We have learned He loved us so much that He died upon the cross to pay the price for our sins. God raised Jesus from the dead, and now Jesus is waiting for us to choose Him. Then, we will have His presence and power through our prayers. Dear friend, I will lead you in a prayer if you are ready to receive Him. This is the greatest decision of your life.

You can pray this prayer:

Jesus, I confess to You that I am a sinner. I'm asking You to forgive me for my sins. I do believe You are the Son of God, and I thank You for dying to pay the cost of my sin. I know God raised You from the dead, and You are alive.

I ask You now to be my Lord and Savior forever. I want Your Holy Spirit to live in me. I no longer will have to struggle alone in this world. I choose You to be with me always here on earth; and I will be with you someday in heaven. Thank You for saving me. In the name of Jesus, I pray. Amen

As I write this, I have a huge smile on my face just thinking about you making this decision. I realize a sense of urgency to finish this project, so that I can get this book to you in order for you to know of the help and power available. I believe that as you prayed this prayer, angels in heaven were celebrating! I am confident that readers of this book who have already prayed this prayer in their past understand the value of the pause.

At the end of the book, you will find information about my website. If you have just accepted Jesus, I especially encourage you to visit it. You will find some information on the next steps in your walk with the Creator. For everyone, there will be a list of other recommended resources, an opportunity to request prayer, and more.

Before we move on from the results of our search for answers on prayer, praise, presence, and power, I would like to share a story. As you have learned from my writing already, accepting Jesus doesn't ensure the absence of trouble during our lives on earth. Accepting Him does mean, as I said before, that we now have someone to whom we can take our troubles, someone who can battle for us. We have God's Holy Spirit, who can give us comfort, hope, and even joy. I have also learned that God does not always answer our prayers the way we might expect or hope. Sometimes we ask and He says "No" or "Not now."

In 2000, when I went for a regular mammogram, the doctor saw something that looked suspicious. I was immediately scheduled for a biopsy. I prayed and asked God to let the test results prove there was nothing wrong with me. Instead, the biopsy confirmed I had breast cancer, and I was scheduled for surgery to be followed by chemotherapy. The attempt to save my beloved family members was put on hold.

Self-Evident Truth

Romans 8:28: "And we know that in all things God works for the good of those who love him, who have been called according to his purpose."

It was during the trial of cancer that I finally learned of God's presence. Before then, I prayed, but I wrongly thought I prayed to a God who was far away. I started reading God's Word more than I ever had, and I finally learned the truth about prayer, praise, presence, and power. I hope that in sharing, I can help someone learn this lesson an easier way.

God heard my cries for help. I believe He may have allowed me to endure this trial in order for me to learn from His truths what I desperately needed to know, so that He could give me a better life. Perhaps He even allowed this trial in order that I would learn to trust Him with my marriage and children, so that He could save them.

God sees everything at once—from the beginning to the end. I believe our lives are similar to a puzzle. Some pieces may not make sense when we look at them; cancer and surgery made no sense to me. God, however, sees the whole puzzle. He could see how this nonsensical piece was an important one in His perfect plan for my life. When this ugly piece was put in its place, it fit where it should in order to form a more beautiful picture or life. This life with more peace and rest and hope was one for which I longed. I started learning to trust the Puzzle Maker.

The Puzzle Maker

God works in life
In so many ways;
Held in His hands
Are all of my days.

Like a puzzle, He places
Each piece as it should—
Some pieces seem wrong,
But He makes them good.

The picture He saw
Before the day of my birth
Was a life filled with purpose,
A picture of worth.

The pieces are many,
And He lets me choose
Which ones to deny
And which ones to use.

Sometimes I choose wrong.
Then, nothing will fit;
I try on my own
But nowhere I get.

To the Puzzle Maker I turn,
Regret in my heart;
He forgives me and loves me
And gives a new start.

A chance for a puzzle
Made with His hands;
A chance for a life—
A life of good plans.

The days are just pieces,
The good and the bad,
But all work in the plan
Of my puzzle He had.

I trust Him to finish
The work He began;
I trust the Puzzle Maker
And I trust His plan.

—Ricki Elks

Chapter 6

A Roadblock Called Unforgiveness

Turning a train around and getting it onto the right track can take time. However, when the train is in position and moving, it can quickly pick up momentum. Once my eyes had been opened to the need for change, once I had made the decision to learn truths, once I had taken those first steps in faith, it was amazing to see how change became progressively easier. The Bible I had once found difficult to read became not only easier to comprehend but also enjoyable and comforting. The Scriptures I had learned began to come to mind at the exact times I needed to hear their wisdom and encouragement. The Holy Spirit, who had once sounded like something of fiction, became to me a real, ever-present, helpful companion.

I soon became aware of other changes I needed to make. There was someone in my life I needed to forgive. I believe the words of the Creator and a prompting of my ever-present companion made me aware of the roadblock that unforgiveness was causing to my progress and my peace.

I had not forgiven a certain person, who I'll refer to as Katie. Although I would make a sincere effort to think excellent, praiseworthy thoughts, angry ones about her would sometimes sneak into my mind. After some resistance, I finally turned to the Creator. It was profound where His guidance took me. Once I reached the surprise ending of this search, I decided to pick up a pen and write the story. Perhaps this is something for you.

The Story of Three Women

Katie

Her name is Katie. Okay, so, it's not really Katie. What is it they say—"The names have been changed to protect the innocent"? Although she may not be innocent, we'll still use an alias.

I found myself deep in thought about Katie. You know that deep-in-thought place, such as where you drive home from the grocery store and later can't recall the drive. Actually, being deep in thought was more like a battle, a one-sided battle with me on the attack. How dare she do the things she had done! How dare she hurt the people I loved! How dare she … Well, you get it—I was down on Katie!

Then the next thought entered my head. Actually, it was a thought about my thoughts. To be exact, I recalled a verse from the Bible that centered on thoughts: "Finally, brothers and sisters, whatever is true, whatever is noble, whatever is right, whatever is pure, whatever is lovely, whatever is admirable—if anything is excellent or praiseworthy—think about such things" (Philippians 4:8). Upon recalling that verse, my response was, "Hey, these points about Katie are true and accurate!" Then, I had to admit, as

I contemplated on the words "noble, pure, lovely," that I couldn't defend my thinking. And when I got to "praiseworthy," I hung my head.

I argued with the Author of the verse by thinking, "But Katie *is* really bad! She's hopeless! I've tried to help her...."

The only answer I got from the Author was a repeat of the verse: "Finally, brothers and sisters, whatever is true, whatever is noble, whatever is right, whatever is pure, whatever is lovely, whatever is admirable—if anything is excellent or praiseworthy—think about such things." I got it—the Author was not happy with my thinking!

The next day, I found no comfort as I recalled my anger with Katie and my attempt to justify it to the Creator. At this point there was another verse on my mind, the words of Jesus found in Matthew 22:39, when Jesus shared the second-most-important command. It was to "love your neighbor as yourself."

Was I loving Katie as I loved myself? The answer was easy. "No!" Truly, *I didn't even like her.* I thought, "She is selfish. She is spoiled. She is critical. She is...." In short, I had to at least admit I did not love Katie as I loved myself. Again, I tried to justify my feelings to the Creator, thinking, "But she has mocked my faith. She has lied to me. She has said mean things to me and about me."

And there it was again—His Word, facing me with uncomfortable truth, like a mirror when I'm without makeup and having a bad-hair day: "But I tell you, love your enemies and pray for those who persecute you" (Matthew 5:44). It was there in black and white, sealed in red: my attitude about Katie was wrong.

Mary

Her name was Mary. While my mind and heart were sorting through my feelings about Katie, for some reason, I kept thinking about Mary. You've probably heard about Mary Magdalene. Why was she on my mind? Was there something about her I needed to know? I decided to read everything the Bible had to say about her. It took me less than thirty minutes.

Mary Magdalene was there that Friday, near the cross along with Jesus' mother and aunt, when Jesus was crucified (John 19:25). That evening, there arrived a man named Joseph, a rich man from Arimathea. He received the body of Jesus, prepared it, placed it in Joseph's own new tomb and sealed it with a large stone. Mary Magdalene was there, sitting opposite the stone (Matthew 27:61). On Saturday, she worked with the other women preparing spices and perfumes to be used for the final preparation of the body of Jesus the next day (Luke 23:56). Early Sunday morning, Mary Magdalene was one of two women who visited the tomb of Jesus and found that the stone had been removed from the entrance. (Matthew 28:1) Also, at the tomb that morning, it was Mary Magdalene and her companion to whom an angel said, "Do not be afraid, for I know that you are looking for Jesus, who was crucified. He is not here; He has risen, just as He said. Come and see the place where He lay." (Matthew 28:5-6) Yes, Mary Magdalene was one of the two women who hurried from the tomb, filled with joy, to tell the disciples the great news (Matthew 28:8).

The gospel of John tells us that it was Mary Magdalene who was the first to hear Jesus speak after His resurrection (John 20:15–16). The *first* to hear Jesus speak! He found her crying and asked, "Woman, why are you crying? Who is it you are looking for?" At first she did not know it was He, but "Jesus said to her, 'Mary.'" When He spoke her name, she *knew* it was Jesus. He spoke her name! Mary Magdalene was indeed special to Jesus. There is no doubt in my mind.

There is one bit of information on Mary I had forgotten. It is the first account of Mary Magdalene in the Gospels. Luke

8:1–3 mentions some women who were supporting Jesus and His disciples as they "traveled from one town and village to another, proclaiming the good news of the kingdom of God." Among these women, Luke says, was "Mary (called Magdalene) from whom seven demons had come out." What? Seven? *Demons?* It's mentioned here almost matter-of-factly. Then, the next mention of her by name is when Jesus is being crucified. What a changed life—from a situation that must have seemed hopeless to being on a first-name basis with the King of Kings!

With a renewed mind, I reread John 20:15: "Woman, why are you crying? Who is it you are looking for?" Again, my thoughts were on Katie. Surely, at times she must have cried. It was evident she was looking for someone or something as she went from man to man and drug to drug. If only she could meet Jesus, she would find what her soul desires. Katie *is indeed* special to Jesus. I have asked my Father to forgive me for my thoughts; and I have replaced them with prayers of faith, prayers that Katie, like Mary Magdalene, will hear Jesus say her name and will recognize her Lord.

Ricki

Her name is Ricki (that's me). It was Wednesday night at church. Just the day before, I had finished writing about Katie and Mary and the lesson God had spoken to me through His Word. Our music director was leading us in praise to the Lord through song. The song was Jared Anderson's "Amazed." I was singing with my eyes closed (helps to keep me focused), "Lord, I'm amazed by you; Lord, I'm amazed by you...." A scene appeared in my mind. In the scene, it's me, not Mary, in that dusty place on that glorious Sunday. It's my name Jesus speaks: "Ricki." And He asks *me*, "Woman, why are you crying? Who are you looking for?"

I opened my eyes and continued to sing, "How You love me!" Immediately, I understood. I, too, am on a first-name basis with the King of Kings! Mary Magdalene's relationship was no more special to Him than mine. Actually, in my relationship with the Lord, I have an advantage. When Mary left Jesus to take the message to the disciples, He was no longer with her. When I go down life's roads, He is always with me. Perhaps now, with this beautiful reminder, I will be quicker to respond in love to the next Katie I encounter.

The Beginning—And the End—Of Forgiveness

Unforgiveness is dangerous and usually has two companions: judging and anger. If my life was now a train on the right track heading in the right direction, these negative mindsets were three sticks of dynamite attached to the tracks up ahead. It was only a matter of time before they destroyed me. I am grateful for the prompting of the Counselor within my heart. My attitude was wrong, and I was unable to move forward until the roadblock—this deadly trio—was removed. I searched the Scriptures and found the truths I needed to hear.

In the eighteenth chapter of Matthew, Jesus tells a story to emphasize the importance of forgiveness. The story is of a king who took pity on one of his servants who owed him a great debt. The king showed the servant mercy and forgave him of all of his debts. Afterward, that same servant went to one of his fellow servants and demanded he pay back the debt he owed. This fellow servant begged to be shown mercy; however, he was shown none. Instead, he was thrown into prison. The king heard what had happened and called the first servant in. "You wicked servant," he said, "I canceled all that debt of yours because you begged me to. Shouldn't you have had mercy on your fellow servant just as I had on you?" The story continues by telling us "in anger, his master handed him over to the jailers to be tortured, until he should pay back all he owed." At the end of the story, Jesus says, "This is how my heavenly Father will treat each of you unless you forgive your brother or sister from your heart."

It became clear to me that the dangerous trio of unforgiveness, judging, and anger was present in my life. Not only did I need to forgive Katie and others who had negatively influenced and hurt my loved ones, but also I needed to forgive my loved ones who had disappointed and hurt me.

And finally, I realized, I needed to forgive myself. I had made so many mistakes with my family. It had taken me so long to learn what my loved ones needed me to learn. Forgiving myself was harder than forgiving anyone else, even Katie. As I pondered the truths of the Creator, however, my eyes were opened to awareness—this trio must be removed from my heart and the tracks ahead.

Self-Evident Truths

Romans 2:1: "You, therefore, have no excuse, you who pass judgment on someone else, for at whatever point you judge another, you are condemning yourself, because you who pass judgment do the same things."

Luke 6:37: "Do not judge, and you will not be judged. Do not condemn, and you will not be condemned. Forgive, and you will be forgiven."

Matthew 6:14: "For if you forgive other people when they sin against you, your heavenly Father will also forgive you."

Colossians 3:13: "Bear with each other and forgive one another if any of you has a grievance against someone. Forgive as the Lord forgave you."

Here is one more beautiful truth recorded in the gospel of Luke. It is a truth spoken by Jesus after He had been beaten and mocked and was hanging upon the cross as a sacrifice to save us: "Father, forgive them, for they do not know what they are doing" (Luke 23:34).

If we do not learn the value of forgiveness, if we do not stop judging, if we do not control our anger, these negative heart attitudes will destroy us. Also, we need to learn to forgive to be an example for others and to be obedient to the Creator who forgave us!

Chapter 7

Treasure of Truths

It has been over a decade since I visited that bookstore looking for a book with the answers on how to help my son. Since I didn't find the book for which I was looking, I pulled an old book off my shelf at home, the Bible, the Word of the Creator. This recorded Word of heaven and earth's maker became my favorite resource. Within its pages, I did find the answers I needed. To my surprise, I also uncovered within its pages a "treasure of truths" I never expected to find. I have had over one hundred hours of counseling and have read multiple books by various authors, but what if I had only had that one book? Could I have obtained the wisdom I needed? Were the answers to all my questions there waiting for me to discover?

I decided to do an experiment with the Creator's Word. I had noticed that in my counseling and in books written by experts, certain words and phrases were repeatedly used in regard to addiction and relationships with addicts. I decided to make a list. As we look together at these terms, you will see I have started with definitions provided by *Merriam–Webster Online, 2015*. Then, we'll see what treasures God's Word has to offer; I call those *treasured truths*.

1. Addiction

The *Merriam–Webster's* definitions for *addiction* include the following:

- A strong and harmful need to regularly have something (such as a drug) or do something (such as gamble)
- An unusually great interest in something or a need to do or have something.

Let's compare a relevant truth from the Bible.

Treasured Truth

2 Peter 2:17–19: "These people are springs without water and mists driven by a storm. Blackest darkness is reserved for them. For they mouth empty, boastful words and, by appealing to the lustful desires of the flesh, they entice people who are just escaping from those who live in error. They promise them freedom, while they themselves are slaves of depravity—for 'people are slaves to whatever has mastered them.'"

I think that passage has one of the best descriptions of addiction: "people are slaves to whatever has mastered them." It was easy for me to see how this was applicable to my loved ones who were slaves to alcohol or drugs. It took me longer to see how it could also apply to a mother. The first of the Ten Commandments given to Moses by God is "You shall have no other gods before me" (Exodus 20:3). Perhaps, in its simplest form addiction could be defined as anything we put before God. When a so-called religious man asked Jesus what was the greatest commandment, Jesus answered, "'Love the Lord your God with all your heart and with all your soul and with all your mind.' This is the first and greatest commandment. And the second is like it: 'Love your neighbor as yourself.' All the Law and the Prophets hang on these two commandments" (Matthew 22:34–40). An addict will love the substance, activity, or person first—before God and all others.

Treasured Truths

1 Peter 5:8: "Be alert and of sober mind. Your enemy the devil prowls around like a roaring lion looking for someone to devour."

Romans 6:16: "Don't you know that when you offer yourselves to someone as obedient slaves, you are slaves of the one you obey-whether you are slaves to sin, which leads to death, or to obedience, which leads to righteousness?"

2. Boundaries

In defining *boundaries, Merriam–Webster's* says:

Unofficial rules about what should not be done; limits that define acceptable behavior.

If you read the story of creation in Genesis, you will see that the Creator believed in physical and behavioral boundaries. He separated the light from the darkness; He separated the water from the land, and so on. In the second chapter of Genesis, God creates man. On that same day (perhaps immediately) God gives man boundaries and warns him of the consequences if the boundaries are broken: "You are free to eat from any tree in the garden; but you must not eat from the tree of the knowledge of good and evil, for when you eat from it you will certainly die" (Genesis 2:16–17).

One of the earliest Scriptures I remember hearing from the Bible was the Twenty-third Psalm. As a child, I thought it was simply a story of a shepherd taking care of his sheep. Later I realized it was also a story of my Shepherd taking care of me. This beautiful psalm contains a wonderful explanation of boundaries. The rod spoken of in the fourth verse can be used to prod a lamb forward; the staff can be used to keep a lamb from going off the side of the desired path. A shepherd used these boundary tools to protect the sheep. Without boundaries, there would be chaos; with them there could be rest and comfort.

Treasured Truth

Psalm 23:4: " ...Your rod and your staff, they comfort me."

I gave my children boundaries along with warnings of the consequences if they got outside those established guidelines. However, I often did not follow through with those consequences. "Perhaps," I would reason, "I was being too harsh." Also, I would feel punished myself as our schedule or activities were affected by the children's punishment. Whatever my rationale, I might lessen or do away with the consequence entirely. Did I think I was being a loving mother showing grace? Was I instead a weak mother, a pleaser, who desired approval from my children? Rather than fostering peace, was I instead establishing the foundation for chaos that would only grow with time?

Treasured Truth

Proverbs 3:11–12: "My son, do not despise the LORD's discipline, and do not resent his rebuke, because the LORD disciplines those he loves, as a father the son he delights in."

A key word in the verse above is *loves*. The verse does not say the Lord disciplines those subservient individuals over whom He has power. Boundaries are set because of love, and a loving discipline follows when they are ignored.

Regretfully, when my children were little, I did quite a bit of yelling and threatening without consistently following through when boundaries were disregarded. I continued this destructive behavior when I was dealing with my adult child who was dealing with the stronghold of addiction. I would set limits with consequences if they were not followed, but then I would cave in when faced with arguing and artful manipulation. I understand now that my failure to stand firm on set boundaries came from a place of weakness, insecurity, neediness; that is, selfish and destructive behavior, not the love my child needed. My child needed a strong, self-assured shepherd with rod and staff in hand.

I did finally read the self-evident truths, the treasured words of the Creator, with my eyes open. It was not too late to set boundaries in my life. Now, the boundaries do the work, and I can rest.

3. Codependency

Merriam–Webster's says:

> A psychological condition or relationship in which
> a person is controlled or manipulated by another
> who is affected by a pathological condition (as an
> addiction to alcohol or heroin).

Treasured Truth

Proverbs 3:5–6: "Trust in the LORD
with all your heart and lean not on your own
understanding; in all your ways submit to him,
and he will make your paths straight."

The above truth became my tool to test my interactions with
others. Was I using my own understanding to help those I loved,
or was I trusting God with *all* of my heart? Was I pointing them
to the Creator for answers, or was I trying to *be* their answer? On
the other side of the question, was I looking to a person to fill
voids in my life that only God could fill?

Treasured Truth

Jeremiah 17:5–6: "This is what the LORD
says: 'Cursed is the one who trusts in man, who
draws strength from mere flesh and whose heart
turns away from the LORD. That person will be
like a bush in the wastelands; they will not see
prosperity when it comes. They will dwell in the
parched places of the desert in a salt land where
no one lives.'"

Even though this verse says "Cursed is the one who trusts in man," I am quite certain that includes putting trust in mothers, too, and mothers putting too much trust in themselves. There were times my children said, "Mom, I can always come to you, and I know you will be there to help me. You are the best!" I must confess hearing these words made me feel good, but I was wrong. I am not saying parents can never help their children, but I became aware of my own needy pride. I learned to be quicker to say, "I know God will help you with this problem. I promise to pray." (Then, I *did* pray.) There were times when this was not a popular response, but the results were obvious—my loved ones became more confident in themselves and did learn to trust in the Lord, not their mother. Also, the more I trusted God and accepted His love for me the less I needed acceptance and approval from others who were incapable of providing what I sought.

The unexpected bonus was that the less I tried to be the answer to their problems the more love and respect I received from them. What peace comes from stopping the unhealthy cycle of codependency!

4. Consequence

Merriam—Webster's says:

> Something that happens as a result of a particular action or set of conditions.

The Bible is full of verses and stories on consequences. Had I missed these truths over the years? Did I, like some of those individuals throughout the history of the Bible, think I (and my loved ones) could somehow escape consequences?

Treasured Truth

Galatians 6:7: "Do not be deceived: God cannot be mocked. A man reaps what he sows."

Did I ever try to mock God by "helping" my children avoid reaping negative things after they had sown negative things? Over the years, did I ever try to hold off the wall of negative consequences from crashing upon them? How often did I yell, criticize, and threaten to take action, but did nothing? If so, God was not mocked—the crashing eventually happened. Is a delayed consequence more severe than one that happens immediately? From experience, I would say, "Most definitely."

I love the story of David. In 1 Samuel 13:14 and in Acts 13:22, the Bible tells us that David was a man after God's own heart. If you read many of the psalms written by David, you can get an idea of why God may have loved David so much—perhaps because David clearly loved God so much. The most famous story of David is his battle against Goliath in 1 Samuel 17. David did not go after this giant simply for David's own glory; he faced the giant in "the name of the Lord Almighty," and he made it clear "the battle is the Lord's." David loved and served God, and David received positive consequences: he had many successes; he was highly respected and admired; and he even became king of Israel.

Then, we are told, David commits sins, and the negative consequences begin. David sleeps with Bathsheba, the wife of another man, and a child is conceived from this adulterous union. To hide this sin, David sins again. He orders Bathsheba's husband to be placed in a battle position that ensures his death. The consequences for David's wrong choices include the death of the baby as well as tragic conduct by David's other children who turn on and sin against each other. Eventually, King David's life is threatened by one of his own sons, and the king is driven out of his kingdom. He is broken as he reaps what he has sown.

David does confess his sin. He continues to love God and praise Him until the end of David's life. And eventually there are some positive consequences for David.

The story of David tells me that the Creator, who loved David greatly, allowed David to suffer negative consequences. If God, in His ultimate wisdom, understands the necessity of consequences, wouldn't I be foolish to try to help my loved ones escape the consequences of their actions?

Treasured Truth

Isaiah 59:2: "But your iniquities have separated you from your God; your sins have hidden his face from you, so that he will not hear."

The worst consequence of sin for David and for our loved ones (or ourselves) is being separated from God and to have His face hidden from us. When I fail, I must face my consequences. I must confess my own failures and seek God's forgiveness. I cannot do this for those I love—they must face their own consequences and seek His forgiveness for themselves!

5. Denial

Merriam–Webster's says:

A psychological defense mechanism in which confrontation with a personal problem or with reality is avoided by denying the existence of the problem or reality.

There were many times I was in denial about my son's addiction. It was easier to believe that the change in him was due to the stress of school or life than to believe that the one I loved was using drugs. It was easier to believe that jobs were just hard to find or that bosses were unfair than to admit the issue was drugs. How many times did I blame friends, teachers, my son's biological father, my husband, and myself, but not my child?

Treasured Truths

> **Jeremiah 5:21:** "Hear this, you foolish and senseless people, who have eyes but do not see, who have ears but do not hear:"

> **1 John 3:18:** "Dear children, let us not love with words or speech but with actions and in truth."

Returning to the story of Adam and Eve in Genesis, we will find the first recorded act of denial, which began with a lie from the Enemy. "You will not certainly die, the serpent said to the woman. For God knows that when you eat from it your eyes will be opened, and you will be like God, knowing good and evil" (Genesis 3:4–5). In denial of the truth, Eve, and then Adam, ate the forbidden fruit. The consequences were eternal.

Living in denial helps no one—not yourself, not the ones you love. My simple definition for living in denial would be "living a lie." There is only one key to unlock the bondage of this existence—*the truth!*

Treasured Truth

> **John 8:32:** "Then you will know the truth, and the truth will set you free."

6. Enabler

Merriam–Webster's says:

> One that enables another to achieve an end;
> especially: one who enables another to persist in
> self-destructive behavior (as substance abuse) by
> providing excuses or by making it possible to
> avoid the consequences of such behavior.

I am certain there were many who could see I was enabling my son to live his self-destructive lifestyle. I was running from one counselor to another asking, "How can I save my son?"

I can imagine they all wanted to shout, "Stop being an enabler!"

In Genesis 27, the story is told of how Jacob deceived his father in order to get the blessing that was supposed to go to Jacob's older brother, Esau. It is a story of lies and manipulation, but Jacob was not the only deceiver. His mother, Rebekah, played an active role in the deception. She enabled Jacob to deceive his father by helping Jacob accomplish his foul deed. She was equally guilty if not more so—she was the parent! As they carried out the act, Jacob had concerns of being caught. I find Rebekah's answer to console him quite alarming. She said, "My son, let the curse fall on me ..."

How many parents are allowing the curse to fall upon themselves as they provide comfortable shelter, cable television, transportation, cell phones, and more to their children who are living a self-destructive lifestyle? The curse, however, falls not just on the parent but also on the child they love. How many parents are like I was—feeling like they are watching their child drown, while remaining clueless that they are the attached heavy weight pulling the child under?

Treasured Truths

1 Corinthians 1:31: "Therefore, as it is written: 'Let the one who boasts boast in the Lord.'"

Proverbs 22:6: "Start children off on the way they should go, and even when they are old they will not turn from it."

If in the past, like me, you didn't get this exactly right, you can begin today.

7. Hit Bottom

Regarding "hit," *Merriam–Webster's* says:

To touch (something or someone) in a forceful or violent way after moving at a high speed.

Regarding "bottom," *Merriam–Webster's* says:

The lowest part, point or level of something.

To form a definition of hitting bottom in regard to addiction, we could use a combination of the two above definitions and say, "Hitting bottom is moving forcefully and violently until contact is made with the lowest conceivable situation in life." Hitting bottom can be the "manure times" we covered previously. The bottom can look different for different people, but it is never a place anyone would choose. For some, bottoming out can be like manure; for others, it may be more like being hit by the manure truck!

Jesus gave the best story I have ever heard on an individual hitting bottom. Let's listen to Jesus tell the story.

Jesus continued: "There was a man who had two sons. The younger one said to his father, 'Father, give me my share of the estate.' So he divided his property between them.

Not long after that, the younger son got together all he had, set off for a distant country and there squandered his wealth in wild living. After he had spent everything, there was a severe famine in that whole country, and he began to be in need. So he went and hired himself out to a citizen of that country, who sent him to his fields to feed pigs. He longed to fill his stomach with the pods that the pigs were eating, but no one gave him anything.

When he came to his senses, he said, 'How many of my father's hired servants have food to spare, and here I am starving to death! I will set out and go back to my father and say to him: Father, I have sinned against heaven and against you. I am no longer worthy to be called your son; make me like one of your hired servants.' So he got up and went to his father ..." (Luke 15:11–20)

It seems, to say the least, that the young man was not honoring his father in asking early for the young man's share of his inheritance and leaving for a distant land. He displayed a lack of wisdom when he squandered the money and lived a wild lifestyle. Then came his bottom: hanging out with pigs that had more to eat than he did. Finally, we see the value of "bottom"— the young rebel realized his mistake, and he made the decision to repent. Furthermore, "he got up and went to his father." Any parent with a prodigal longs for that day.

In thunderstorms, when the temperature of the ground contrasts greatly with the temperature of the atmosphere, conditions are ideal for forming a tornado. So, too, hitting bottom can create the best possible condition for change. Suddenly, the pain of the comfortable, familiar addiction or codependent relationship is greater than the pain and fear of change.

It must have been hard for the wayward son to go to his father and admit he had been wrong and apologize, but living with pigs was worse. As we continue to read in Luke 15, we find the son returning to his father and a happy end to the parable. I must, however, ask myself a question: "How would the story have ended if the father had gone to that foreign land and asked the son to come home before the son had hit bottom?" Perhaps the son's anger would have turned toward his father instead of himself, thus blocking the progress to a place of repentance.

I'm not a huge fan of boxing, but I have occasionally found myself in front of a television with friends, watching some championship match. I remember watching one boxer take a beating. The announcer kept saying he didn't know why one punch after another didn't knock this fighter out. The hard punches continued for what seemed an eternity until the boxer fell face forward to the mat. That's how my bottom came to me. My daughter was in a codependent relationship with a manipulative man and left the state. I was diagnosed with breast cancer, had a mastectomy, was treated with chemotherapy, and lost all of my hair. My son was expelled from high school a few months before graduation and was soon arrested, the first of many times.

I finally said out loud, "I must be doing something wrong." Like the prodigal, I got up and ran to my Father. I began to pray as I had never prayed before. I began to realize the Creator had answers I needed right there in His Word. More than anything else, I finally realized that the Holy Spirit was actually present with me every minute of every day. I do not look upon the bottom of my life with remorse, but instead, with gratitude for the jolt that resulted in my first step toward change.

Treasured Truth

Ecclesiastes 3:1–7: "There is a time for everything, and a season for every activity under the heavens ... a time to tear and a time to mend ..."

8. Letting Go

Regarding "Let go," *Merriam–Webster's* says:

To relax or release one's hold

I remember when my oldest child was a little over two years old and I was visiting a friend who lived in an upstairs apartment. To reach the living room where we gathered, one had to climb a wooden stairway that was steep and treacherous and then walk through a hallway. We were all keeping a careful eye on this adventurous two-year-old, or at least we thought we were. We must have all lost focus at the same time. I looked around, and my little Renee was gone. My heart stopped.

I moved quickly but cautiously out of the living room into the hall. There she was, just where I had feared she would be— at the edge of the top of the staircase. She turned around and looked at me. I tried to appear calm, because I knew if she sensed me coming after her she would turn to run, and one step away from me could be her last. I smiled and asked her if she wanted a cookie. In that context, turning away from the staircase was her idea, and she ran to me. I cried and hugged her, but she just wanted her cookie.

What do we do when we watch an adult we love standing dangerously close to a treacherous edge? Do we offer them a cookie of some sort? Does that work with addicts? Just as with my infant daughter, I believe, turning away from the edge must be *their* idea. However, I have found that bottoms work better than cookies.

I can remember how hard I tried one Christmas to make everything so special that my son would turn away from the dangerous edge to which his destructive stronghold had taken him. It worked for a short time—long enough for a few Christmas photos where we all posed normally. When I look at those pictures now, I can see the sadness in my son's eyes, and I am aware of the desperation in mine. It was only a matter of hours before my son was again standing by that edge.

I met a woman once who said she and her husband had to sell their home because of the money they spent on lawyers and fines due to their son's drug problem. They spent the last of their savings to get their son into a court-ordered rehab. If her son would complete the program, he would not go to jail. To help her son avoid such a devastating fall, she had offered him a type of cookie—the promise of a new car if he completed the program. She confessed she would have to borrow the money. I never saw the woman again, but I'm quite confident her cookie did not have the power to motivate her son.

Letting go—"to relax or release one's hold." How can we let go when we know our precious ones could fall? Perhaps it would be easier if we realized there is no power in cookies and we are not strong enough to hold on indefinitely to those we love. There *is*, however, power in letting go. Remember when I shared about the counselor who told me the best way to save my son was to let him go (by no longer allowing him to live in our home)? Do you remember I responded to his advice by listing all the possible negatives that could occur if I followed his recommendation? Then, the counselor said that something bad *could* happen but letting my son go was the *only* way he would ever get better.

The counselor had the answer to the question "What do we do when we watch an adult we love stand dangerously close to a treacherous edge?" He also knew the Truth who was behind the truth; we let go of our loved one, *but* we do so *knowing* that the unseen hands of the Creator are ready to pull His children to safety if they will only reach out to Him. Could it be they will never be able to grab onto those powerful, saving hands as long as our hands are in the way?

In Luke 15, the father of the prodigal let his son go. He even gave his son the inheritance he had requested. The father didn't run after the son begging him to stay. He didn't even seek him out in that foreign land and bribe him with a "cookie" to come home. He let him go, and he waited. I believe that while he waited, he prayed. The son did fall—he fell into a pit of swine. However, that is where he found the strength to change and go back to his father.

LETTING GO Is Letting Go of Our Control

Treasured Truth

Proverbs 3:5–6: "Trust in the Lord with all your heart and lean not on your own understanding; in all your ways submit to him, and he will make your paths straight."

LETTING GO Is Letting Go of Our Bitterness and Anger

Treasured Truth

Ephesians 4:31: "Get rid of all bitterness, rage and anger, brawling and slander, along with every form of malice."

LETTING GO Is Letting Go of Our Pride

Treasured Truth

1 Peter 5:6: "Humble yourselves, therefore, under God's mighty hand, that he may lift you up in due time."

LETTING GO Is Letting Go of the Past

Treasured Truth

2 Corinthians 5:17: "Therefore, if anyone is in Christ, the new creation has come: The old has gone, the new is here!"

LETTING GO Is Letting the Creator Take Your Worries

Treasured Truth

1 Peter 5:7: "Cast all your anxiety on him because he cares for you."

LETTING GO Is *Letting the Creator Fight the Battle*

Treasured Truths

Romans 12:19: "Do not take revenge, my dear friends, but leave room for God's wrath, for it is written: 'It is mine to avenge; I will repay,' says the Lord."

1 Samuel 17:47: " ...for the battle is the LORD's ..."

LETTING GO Is *Resting and Receiving God's Peace*

Treasured Truth

Philippians 4:6–7: "Do not be anxious about anything, but in every situation, by prayer and petition, with thanksgiving, present your requests to God. And the peace of God, which transcends all understanding, will guard your hearts and your minds in Christ Jesus."

More Than Anything, LETTING GO *Is Trusting the Creator!*

Treasured Truths

Jeremiah 29:11: "For I know the plans I have for you," declares the Lord, "plans to prosper you and not to harm you, plans to give you hope and a future."

Romans 8:28: "And we know that in all things God works for the good of those who love him, who have been called according to his purpose."

John 10:9–10: "I am the gate; whoever enters through me will be saved. They will come in and go out, and find pasture. The thief comes only to steal and kill and destroy; I have come that they may have life, and have it to the full."

For me, letting go was not a one-time event. Sometimes I still catch myself tempted to grab the hand of my precious ones, but I am now quicker to remind myself there are better hands to hold them. Then, grateful for the One who is the Truth, I again let go.

I wrote the following poem, "Commands and Demands," for my youngest daughter when she graduated high school (over eighteen years ago). The poem shows that I was struggling with the thought of letting her go. It does seem, however, I had some awareness that God would take care of her if she would only grab ahold of His hands. The truth is that my commands and demands continued for years before I began to ease my grip. As my eyes were finally opening, my daughter and I made an agreement. If she sensed I was crossing a boundary of respect and calling it help, she would simply lift her pointing finger. I agreed that once she gave the signal, I would stop talking immediately. I must further confess that when this happened it was so hard to stop, because I just *knew* she needed to hear what I had to say. But at such times I have kept quiet because I love my daughter more than my need to save or control. Plus, I reminded myself of those unseen powerful hands that would not grab her unless I got out of His way.

Commands and Demands

Don't play with the fire,
And don't speak to strangers.
Stand back from the edge –
The world's full of dangers.

Look both ways before crossing,
Hold tight to my hand,
Brush twice every day;
Shoulders back when you stand.

I must seem like a sergeant
With all my commands:
Do this; don't do that –
So many demands.

But if you could see inside,
Inside of my heart,
You'd see love and concern
That I've felt from the start.

Tiny hand around my finger,
Eyes that trusted me so
To lead and to teach you
The way you should go.

I made many mistakes
No matter how hard I tried;
Sometimes you fell
And sometimes you cried.

And now it's OVER.
Commands and demands are through.
Just one last time
Let me say to you:

Don't play with the fire,
And don't speak to strangers.
Stand back from the edge –
The world's full of dangers.

Look both ways before crossing,
Hold tight to His hand.
Brush twice every day;
Shoulders back when you stand.

Oh, one more thing: I love you so
much, and I will always love you!

—Ricki Elks

9. One Day at a Time

Do we really need *Merriam—Webster's* for this one? Here is a definition provided by me:

> Not yesterday; not tomorrow; only the twenty-four-hour period of today.

Don't Stir the Pot of the Past

My husband and I were visiting our friends Charlie and Judy. (Reminder: Charlie was a marriage counselor and a substance abuse counselor.) When we met Charlie, we had no idea we would need and often turn to him for advice in both of his areas of expertise. Charlie's wife, Judy, didn't have the certificates hanging on the wall; however, she certainly had an abundance of wisdom and excelled as a friend. During this particular evening, I shared with our friends some challenges we were facing with our children. Then, I started verbalizing my guilt and regrets: "If I hadn't put them through a divorce …"; "If I could have provided more structure …"; "I should have …"; "I could have …" I was beating myself up for my perceived mistakes, and I didn't overlook my husband as I passed out the blame.

Finally, Charlie said, "Let's not waste time on 'woulda, shoulda, coulda.' Let's focus on what we should start doing today." He said people sometimes spend years *stirring the pot of the past* and never move forward. As I have stated before, I'm not a professional counselor, but Charlie was; and he was quite successful. I looked to see if Charlie was in agreement with what the Creator had to say about the past. Here are a few pertinent truths:

Treasured Truths

Isaiah 43:18: "Forget the former things; do not dwell on the past."

Philippians 3:13: " ...But one thing I do: Forgetting what is behind and straining toward what is ahead ..."

Isaiah 43:25: "I, even I, am he who blots out your transgressions, for my own sake, and remembers your sins no more."

I have a feeling I know where Charlie got his wisdom.

A Thief Called Tomorrow

Equally as problematic as the urge to stir the pot of the past was my temptation to dwell on tomorrow. I was so often worrying about tomorrow that I hardly noticed the sun had risen on a new day and then set. Concern for tomorrow was stealing my todays.

"What ifs" consumed much of my life. At times I cried real tears for imaginary "what ifs." How foolish is that? Then, if you add in the fact that most of my "what ifs" revolved around other people over whom I had no control, it is doubly foolish. The Creator has treasured truths on the subject of tomorrow. This one makes the point clearly:

Treasured Truth

Matthew 6:34: "Therefore do not worry about tomorrow, for tomorrow will worry about itself. Each day has enough trouble of it's own."

Why do we not have to worry about tomorrow? The answer is because we have a trustworthy, good Shepherd to lead and help us.

Treasured Truths

John 16:33: "I have told you these thing, so that in me you may have peace. In this world you will have trouble. But take heart! I have overcome the world."

Psalm 31:14–15: "But I trust in you, LORD; I say, 'You are my God.' My times are in your hands; ..."

Psalm 112:7: "They will have no fear of bad news; their hearts are steadfast, trusting in the LORD."

To change my fixation on tomorrow and the trouble and bad news it could bring, I had to be proactive. I began to listen to soothing music and songs that reminded me of God's power and help. I read His Word daily, especially the psalms that reminded me over and over of His loving hands of protection. Sometimes aloud I would quote from the psalms, such as the verses above in Psalm 31: "But I trust in you, Lord ... My times are in your hands ..." I began to pray more confidently, and I could feel His help.

Treasured Truth

Psalm 34:4: "I sought the LORD, and he answered me; he delivered me from all my fears."

Then, I began to replace these thoughts of worry and fear with thoughts of faith. I wrote on a page of my journal a few paragraphs describing my loved ones living happy, productive lives and loving and following God's will. I often would read this proclamation of faith, picturing it happening and considering how I would feel.

Treasured Truth

Hebrews 11:1: "Now faith is confidence in what we hope for and assurance about what we do not see."

Tomorrow became a place only God can see and a place I entrusted (and continue entrusting) to Him. I also continued to remind myself of His promises, and I claimed them for those I loved.

Treasured Truth

Jeremiah 29:11: "'For I know the plans I have for you,' declares the Lord, 'plans to prosper you and not to harm you, plans to give you hope and a future.'"

I gave tomorrow to the Creator.

Today—One Day (This Day) at a Time

When I quit looking back on the past, and when I quit worrying about tomorrow, I found myself present in the moment of today. My clarity of mind was heightened when my focus was directed upon a mere twenty-four hours. Peace and purpose became new acquaintances.

Then, I heard them—the birds in my backyard. There were yellow ones and red ones; there were tiny hummingbirds and giant blue jays. I sometimes lost track of time as I felt the joy of the moment, just watching and listening. Had they always been there? Had I been so busy stirring a pot and entertaining a thief that I had missed them?

Treasured Truth

Psalm 118:24: "The LORD has done it this very day; let us rejoice today and be glad."

When Jesus was teaching His disciples (and us) how to pray, He said we should ask the Father to give us what we need for the day (Luke 11:3). Living one day at a time and knowing we will receive all we need (not want) from the Creator—what security and reason to rest!

Treasured Truth

Luke 11:3: "Give us each day our daily bread."

There were so many gifts waiting for me as I learned to live one day at a time, as I still do.

Treasured Truth

2 Corinthians 6:2: "For he says, 'In the time of my favor I heard you, and in the day of salvation I helped you.' I tell you, now is the time of God's favor, now is the day of salvation."

Jesus promised in John 16:33 that "in this world you will have trouble." Troubles still came into my life, leading to some tough days. Jesus continued to promise in that same verse: "but take heart I have overcome the world." Although the challenges came, I no longer battled alone. In addition to relishing my partnership with the Victor, I was dealing with only *one day*. The sun would soon set, and the next singular day would be a new opportunity for rejoicing and victory. Again, I would wake up to a new morning. I would be able to thank the Father for a new sunrise and another opportunity to hear the birds and praise Him. Then, I would ask Him, "Give me this day my daily bread."

10. Tough Love

Merriam–Webster's says:

Love or affectionate concern expressed in a stern or unsentimental manner (as through discipline) especially to promote responsible behavior.

One day at a grocery store, I watched a young mother dealing with her three-year-old son. Without her permission, he brought her a small bag of chips he really wanted. "No," she said. "It's too close to dinner. Now, go put them back."

He rebutted. "Please. I'm hungry." Again, she said no.

Then, he put it in high gear and added a scream. "Open for me! I want chips!"

The debate between this adult and small child continued for minutes. Then, the three-year-old, in anger, stomped on the bag of chips. The mother, who was clearly frustrated and exhausted, yielded to the miniature giant; she opened the bag for him.

Tough love can be tough. It's easy to point at this mother and shake our heads, but let's not be so quick to judge. She was in a public place dealing with a strong-willed child by herself. She was embarrassed and her anxiety level was climbing. At that moment, her desire for peace was greater than her desire to teach.

However, even when we don't think we are teaching, don't our actions teach or train others how to treat us? Didn't this mother inadvertently teach this little man how to get what he wants? It seems this was not teaching him to respect her. I am reminded of when I would set a boundary and then back down due to my desire for peace. Here's what the Creator has to say:

Treasured Truth

Proverbs 22:6: "Start children off on the way they should go, and even when they are old they will not turn from it."

Since the Creator is our Father, I decided to check out His parenting skills to see if He used tough love. I found a few examples.

I looked back at the story of Adam and Eve in Genesis 3 to see how the Father dealt with His children after they had chosen to listen to the Enemy instead of to obey God's singular demand. I discovered His *tough love* included banishing them from the Garden of Eden where all had been provided for them. After that, they had to endure hard labor, pain, and even death.

I looked in the book of Exodus at the Israelites, God's children who He delivered from bondage in Egypt. God had the gift of the Promised Land waiting for them; however, because of their disobedience, God delayed His gift. The trip, which some say could have taken days, took forty years due to the *tough love* of the Father.

I also looked in the book of Exodus at Moses, who clearly had an especially close relationship with God. In Exodus 3, God chooses Moses to deliver the Israelites. Later, we hear that "The LORD would speak to Moses face to face, as one speaks to a friend" (Exodus 33:11). However, in another chapter, as God passes in front of Moses, God tells Moses that He "does not leave the guilty unpunished" (Exodus 34:7).

Moses would find out later the truth of God's words. In Numbers 20, God gives Moses specific instructions on how to provide water to the Israelites: by speaking to a rock out of which God would pour water. Moses chooses, instead, to strike the rock, and still the desired results happen—water flows. However, because of his disobedience, Moses experiences the *tough love* of his Father. A few verses later, God tells Moses (who has delivered the Israelites out of bondage and led them for forty years) that Moses would not be allowed to enter into the Promised Land. Now, that's *tough love*!

Although my journey through the Word made it clear the Creator did believe in tough love, His priority on the second word of the phrase could not be missed as I turned the pages. The Creator's emphasis throughout the ages has been *love*.

Treasured Truths

John 3:16: "For God so loved the world that he gave his one and only Son, that whoever believes in him shall not perish but have eternal life."

1 Peter 4:8: "Above all, love each other deeply, because love covers over a multitude of sins."

Matthew 22:35–40: "One of them, an expert in the law, tested him with this question: 'Teacher, which is the greatest commandment in the Law?' Jesus replied, '"Love the Lord your God with all your heart and with all your soul and with all your mind." This is the greatest commandment. And the second is like it: "Love your neighbor as yourself." All the Law and the Prophets hang on these two commandments.'"

When I first heard the term *tough love* and then read the *Merriam–Webster's* definition, I misunderstood what it meant. I pictured a tyrant lording over someone with demands. But as I read how the Creator says we should treat the people in our lives, I knew His desire was something entirely opposite. Let's look at some of the Creator's relationship guidelines:

Treasured Truths

1 Corinthians 13:4–7: "Love is patient, love is kind. It does not envy, it does not boast, it is not proud. It does not dishonor others, it is not self-seeking, it is not easily angered, it keeps no record of wrongs. Love does not delight in evil but rejoices with the truth. It always protects, always trusts, always hopes, always perseveres."

Ephesians 6:4: "Fathers, do not exasperate your children; instead, bring them up in the training and instruction of the Lord."

Proverbs 15:1: "A gentle answer turns away wrath, but a harsh word stirs up anger."

Ephesians 5:33: "However, each one of you also must love his wife as he loves himself, and the wife must respect her husband."

Ephesians 6:2: "'Honor your father and mother'—which is the first commandment with a promise ...'"

James 1:19: "My dear brothers and sisters, take note of this: Everyone should be quick to listen, slow to speak and slow to become angry,"

I also looked back to Luke 15 at the story Jesus told of the prodigal son. Jesus tells how the father reacted when his son finally came home: "But while he was still a long way off, his father saw him and was filled with compassion for him; he ran to his son, threw his arms around him and kissed him." Then, Jesus tells us what the father said to his servants, "'Quick! Bring the best robe and put it on him. Put a ring on his finger and sandals on his feet. Bring the fattened calf and kill it. Let's have a feast and celebrate. For this son of mine was dead and is alive again; he was lost and is found.' So they began to celebrate."

There's no record of the father saying, "I told you so!" There's no mention of lectures or listing of mistakes—just celebration. It's a lesson for you and me on how to treat our loved ones when they come home, and it's a lesson on how our heavenly Father loves us.

You may be asking, as I did at first, "Where's the tough love?" I believe we find it at the end of the story, when the older brother questions the fairness of the celebration for his younger brother. The older sibling reminds his father of the devotion and dedication this sibling showed while the younger brother was off making bad choices. "'My son,' the father said, 'you are always with me, and everything I have is yours. But we had to celebrate and be glad, because this brother of yours was dead and is alive again; he was lost and is found.'" Did you notice the father said "and everything I have is yours"? The father didn't plan to give the younger son another inheritance; so, the consequences of the prodigal's actions were not compromised. *Tough love* was subtly noted, but the emphasis, like the emphasis of our Father, was simply *love*!

At the end of my look into the Word of the Creator on this "tough" subject, I had some serious questions to ask myself. I knew I had always loved my children—I rejoiced at their victories and I tasted salt when they cried. Still, did I love them enough to be tough when it was appropriate? Was I tough enough to set boundaries and allow the established consequences to happen even if it meant my children suffered? Did I allow them to grow during their trials? Did I refuse to be manipulated by them? Finally, did I love them enough and was I tough enough to stop trying to be their savior and allow the Savior to do in them what I never could?

Like the mother of the three-year-old I witnessed that day, I had made disciplinary mistakes as I raised my children. I, too, often set a boundary but allowed debate, tantrums, and manipulation to wear on me until I caved in to the demands. I was not always quick to listen and slow to speak, and my answers were often far from gentle. I had no idea of what I was teaching my children by my conduct. I didn't like confrontation, so I sought a peaceful resolution. I was unaware that I was only increasing future confrontations. I would seek peace and seek peace but then explode when it didn't come. I would get weary like the three-year-old's mother with the bag of chips, and I would give my children whatever they wanted just because it seemed easier for the moment. A wise, confident parent who was fortified with the wisdom of the Creator would have set the boundaries and, if necessary, followed through with the tough love of consequences.

As I have said before, I can do nothing about the mistakes of my past. However, I can use these acquired skills in my life today with my grandchildren and in all of my relationships. And with you, I can share what I have learned.

Treasured Truth:

(1 Corinthians 13:4-7) Love is patient, love is kind. It does not envy, it does not boast, it is not proud. It does not dishonor others, it is not self-seeking, it is not easily angered, it keeps no record of wrongs. Love does not delight in evil but rejoices with the truth. It always protects, always trusts, always hopes, always preserves.

Chapter 8

When I'm Weak, I'm Strong!

Almost immediately after I realized I had some changes to make in myself, the questions began to run across my mind. What if I can't change? What if I can't be tough enough? Can I really let go and rest while trusting God? What if I fail?

We all have weaknesses.

Just in case you thought you were perfect, I am sorry to be the one to break this news to you: we all have weaknesses. Some people are natural-born leaders; however, to others they may come across as bossy. Some people have strengths in organizational and analytical skills, but they may struggle with procrastination. There are those individuals who are fun and never meet a stranger, but they may have poor listening habits and appear self-centered. Then, there are also people who are sweet and peaceful; however, they may lean toward the lazy side. Popeye, a famous cartoon character, had a saying he used often: "I yam what I yam!" (To interpret: "I am what I am.") Was Popeye right? Are we stuck with our weaknesses? If we tend to be easily manipulated or controlled, are we just trapped in our personality? On the other hand, if we tend to want to control others, is that just our nature and who we are forever? Obviously, Popeye didn't understand what the Creator could do with our weaknesses.

Self-Evident Truth

2 Corinthians 12:9–10: "But he said to me, 'My grace is sufficient for you, for my power is made perfect in weakness.' Therefore I will boast all the more gladly about my weaknesses, so that Christ's power may rest on me. That is why, for Christ's sake, I delight in weaknesses, in insults, in hardships, in persecutions, in difficulties. For when I am weak, then I am strong."

The above passage is from a letter (now part of the Bible) that God inspired Paul to write to the Corinthians and to you and me. Paul had previously been known as Saul of Tarsus, and he had been out to destroy the church. In the Bible, the book of Acts says Saul would go from house to house dragging men and women from their homes and throwing them into prison for following Jesus. You may have heard the story of how Jesus appeared to Saul as he was on his way to Damascus to persecute more Christians. The amazing story of his transformation is detailed in the ninth chapter of Acts, but, in short, Saul met Jesus and was filled with the Holy Spirit. Unlike the Popeye attitude, Paul demonstrated with his life that he no longer was who he had been; even his name was changed. He dedicated the rest of his life to telling others of the salvation and power available to them.

I had and have my share of weaknesses. As a mother, I was undisciplined and inconsistent. I was fun one minute and yelling the next. I would set rules one day and ignore them the day after. I would proclaim my faith in God, and then I would verbalize my fears. I was only being who I was and embracing my weaknesses. But my children were not getting the secure foundation they needed. Then one day I was walking down my "Damascus road" and the Creator met me there. He said to me (as I read His Word), "My grace is sufficient for you, for my power is made perfect in weakness."

Then I thought, "What an opportunity for power I have in my life, for I certainly have my share of weaknesses!"

The more I read the more I found stories of God's power displayed amid the weaknesses of others. I read of:

> **Moses** (book of Exodus), who expressed his feelings of inadequacy to God when God told Moses to go to Pharaoh and bring the Israelites out of Egypt. Moses said, "I am slow of speech and tongue." God reminded Moses of the power that is made perfect in weakness and said, "Now go; I will help you speak and will teach you what to say."

> **Gideon** (Judges), whose response to the angel of the Lord calling Gideon a "mighty warrior" was to express his lowly opinion of himself. He basically said he came from a bad family and he was the least of them. I read how Gideon's weaknesses, cowardliness, and lack of confidence served to display the perfecting of the power of God. Gideon did become the mighty warrior God had called him to be.

> **Esther** (Esther), who as a young Jewish girl had lost her parents. She was being raised by her cousin. Esther became Queen of Persia, but she was faced with a life-threatening assignment. With God's power overcoming her weaknesses, she saved a nation.

Mary (Luke), who was only a young virgin from Galilee, but when an angel told her "the power of the Most High will overshadow you," she found the strength to accept her assignment to become mother of the Son of God. She was so young and must have had fears of the negativity she would face from her family and friends, but her weakness was made strong. "I am the Lord's servant," Mary answered. "May your word to me be fulfilled."

Peter (Luke, John, Acts), who was a simple fisherman. He could be weak in his faith as well as impulsive and even cowardly at times. But he became a great, respected, and brave leader of the church after being filled with the power of the Holy Spirit.

These examples, and many more, were there for me to see. What God did with the weaknesses of others He could do for you and me. The following passage explains why we can be confident.

Self-Evident Truth

Hebrews 4:14–16: "Therefore, since we have a great high priest who has ascended into heaven, Jesus the Son of God, let us hold firmly to the faith we profess. For we do not have a high priest who is unable to empathize with our weaknesses, but we have one who has been tempted in every way, just as we are—yet he did not sin. Let us then approach God's throne of grace with confidence, so that we may receive mercy and find grace to help us in our time of need."

In the book of Exodus, Moses asks God His name so that Moses can tell the Israelites the name of the one who sent Moses to lead them out of Egypt. So, in Exodus 3:14, God reveals His name to Moses and provides a *self-evident truth* for us.

> God said to Moses, "I AM WHO I AM. This is what you are to say to the Israelites: 'I AM has sent me to you.'"

Popeye's "I yam who I yam" meant Popeye couldn't change; however, the Creator, the true *I AM*, gives you and me the power to be strong when we are weak. My yelling was replaced by quiet strength. My "no" became a true "no," not a place for debates to begin. My anxiety abated. I became stronger than I ever knew I could be.

Self-Evident Truth

Philippians 4:13 (NKJV): "I can do all things through Christ who strengthens me."

The Creator, the true "I Am," gives us the power to be strong when we are weak!

Chapter 9

I Could Not Save, But God Can!

My husband and I love to watch the birds in our backyard. We have a guidebook on birds resting permanently near our kitchen window, next to a pair of binoculars. We especially enjoy watching in the springtime as the parents-to-be busily build their nests. Later it's equally entertaining to watch them fly back and forth as they feed their demanding new little ones.

I was upset one morning after a thunderstorm to find a nest had blown out of our oak tree in the backyard. Lying on the ground next to the nest was a tiny, fragile baby bird, still alive.

I went inside to watch from the window to see if the parents were going to save their little one. Although they expressed their anxiety in loud bird language, they made no attempt to rescue the baby. After peering from my window over the next hour, I decided it was up to me to do the saving.

I slid a piece of paper under the baby bird's limp body, and as gently as possible, I placed it back in the nest. I then put the nest in the tree from which it had fallen. I waited. After a couple of hours, it was obvious that the parents were not returning. I checked the nest. The little bird had died.

I could not save the little bird, and I have never saved anyone!

After seeing that the bird had not survived, I sat on the steps of our deck and began to cry. Somehow the event had opened up a window into my memories. I recalled that my dad told me once that he had started drinking alcohol before his teen years. He had some uncles who thought it was funny to see him get drunk. Life with my alcoholic father was tough at times, to say the least, for all of us, but especially for my mother. As a girl, I thought my job was to help keep the peace. I stood ready to save if necessary.

I also thought of how, at the end of my twenties and as a mother of three, I had become divorced from my children's father. I was determined my children would not suffer. I believed I could save them from the pain and loss. I was wrong. When my children began to walk (sometimes run) in the wrong direction, I ran after them. I ran as hard as I could. I yelled, "Stop!" as loud as I could yell. I loved as best I knew how. But I could not save them.

Looking back now, I can see that only when I ran out of ideas and strength within myself did I look for wise counsel. It was only when I didn't find a book with all the answers at the bookstore that I pulled the Bible off my shelf and began to read. It was only when the doctor said the word *cancer* that I realized I needed to understand more about God's power. Finally, it was only when I realized *I* could not save my loved ones that something began to happen.

During my third month of chemotherapy, my dad and I went for a walk. He said he was amazed at how I walked along so briskly and joyfully at this point in my treatment. This newfound power and peace in me was proving to be more powerful than the cancerous cells and the poison the doctor had injected to destroy them. I shared with my dad about Jesus and His promises. I know our conversation that day was not the only factor that began a change in my dad (only God can save), but I am confident it played a part. Within the year, I received a call—in his mid-seventies, my dad accepted Jesus as his Lord and Savior! Sixty years of control by alcohol ended. My dad became very active in a small country church where the members loved him until he passed away just before his eighty-third birthday.

The more I let go of my daughters the more they amazed me. Without my unsolicited advice, they found their own answers. They began to make better choices and became strong women and incredible mothers. As I let them go, they returned to me, embracing me with the love and respect that can never be gained by control. Any advice they get from me these days is rare and at their request.

My son finally reached his bottom—he lost his freedom and his daughters. His attorney said it could be years before my son would be with his girls. He was broken and began to pray. The answer did not come immediately, but when it did come, many shook their heads and asked, "How did that happen?" The courts allowed Joshua to attend the one-year residential program of Teen Challenge. Joshua spent a year learning the truths of the Creator, and Joshua became a new man. The truth he claims as self-evident is: "Therefore, if anyone is in Christ, the new creation has come: The old has gone, the new is here!" (2 Corinthians 5:17). The son I had watched as he went down for the third time was replaced with a new man who cares for his family and praises his Creator. Chaos was replaced with pleasant surprises, such as the one on Mother's Day when I looked across the church parking lot and saw my son, his wife, and his daughters coming to join me in worshiping the Creator.

My marriage is now what I believe a marriage should be—a union of love and honor where God is first. My misguided focus and false sense of power nearly caused me to miss this blessed relationship. Our favorite times of the day are early morning and just before dusk. You can usually find us in the swing in the backyard. I'm often leaning against Larry's shoulder looking up into the trees. You might hear me say, "Wow! Look at that beautiful blue jay!" We both are so grateful to be where we are today.

Has every prayer been answered? Not yet, but I continue to "knock." When troubles come, as Jesus said they would, I know where to go for help and strength. I have learned how to battle. I continue to read the Word of the Creator, to trust, and to pray. As for my loved ones, God is always there for them, too. As long as they choose Him one day at a time, they will have, as Jesus promised in John 10:10, "life to the full"!

So, I am nobody's savior, but I have a Savior. I no longer spin plates; I simply trust and rest. I gave to God the ones I loved, and He saved *me*. In the poem, "I Could Not Save the Little Bird", I said, "All I can save is me", but God truly gets credit for my rescue, as well. While I rested on Him, miracles happened—and miracles continue even to this day.

This Eagle Was Meant to Soar

There in the eagle's nest
On the mountain peak so high
Was a tiny baby eagle,
Safe and warm and dry.

For his mother sat beside him
Morning, noon, and night;
If danger ever neared him
This mom would surely fight.

Seasons came and passed
And the tiny eagle grew;
The mother eagle on the peak
Knew what she had to do.

She filled their home with stickers,
A pleasant place no more;
For life had more to offer
Than her son had known before.

She pushed him from the nest home;
He flapped and fell in fear,
But just in time she saved him
As the ground came deadly near.

She placed him in the eagle nest
Only to repeat this action more,
Over and over and over
Until her son began to soar.

She watched him spread his mighty
wings,
Saw pride on his eagle face
As he soared the sky and flew so high;
Her son had found his place.

There in the eagle nest
On the mountain peak that night
A little pain in her eagle chest,
But she knew that she was right.

She held him for a season,
But God had for him much more;
God had for him a purpose—
This eagle was meant to soar!

—Ricki Elks

For other recommended resources,
an opportunity to request prayer, and more,
please visit my website:
http://www.rickielks.com.

Printed in the United States
By Bookmasters